Baron Thomas Babington Macaulay,

Macaulay's Lays of Ancient Rome

Baron Thomas Babington Macaulay,

Macaulay's Lays of Ancient Rome

ISBN/EAN: 9783744788564

Printed in Europe, USA, Canada, Australia, Japan

Cover: Foto ©ninafisch / pixelio.de

More available books at **www.hansebooks.com**

LAYS OF ANCIENT ROME

T. B. MACAULAY

MACAULAY'S

LAYS OF ANCIENT ROME

Edited

With Introduction and Notes

by

MOSES GRANT DANIELL

BOSTON, U.S.A.
GINN & COMPANY, PUBLISHERS
The Athenæum Press
1899

PREFACE.

IN preparing notes for this edition of the *Lays*, the editor has had in mind chiefly the needs of the non-classical student, to whom the text presents much that he is not at all familiar with. What any reader needs, in order to derive the greatest satisfaction from the reading, is a clear appreciation of the circumstances and situations as they might appear to a Roman for whom the *Lays* are assumed to have been written. To go further than this, and make the *Lays* a basis for the extended study of Roman history, geography, mythology, and antiquities, would, in the editor's opinion, be a mistake. The author deemed his own introductions to the several *Lays* to be sufficient; but these take for granted a certain amount of knowledge that young readers cannot fairly be assumed to possess; and even the customary explanatory notes, unless inordinately extended, leave something to be desired. One needs to read at some length the accounts that historians have given of Rome in the early days, in order to surround himself with the right atmosphere, so to speak, in which to read the *Lays* with the keenest appreciation. Any good history of Rome that has a good index may be used for the purpose here indicated.

The editor has not often yielded to the ever-present temptation to give the meanings of words that can be found in a dictionary. Some such words need additional explanation or illustration, but in general the student should learn to depend upon his own research.

A map of Etruria and Latium and parts adjacent and a map of early Rome have been provided, with the idea that it is well for the reader to associate a "local habitation" with the names that he encounters, and that maps are better than notes for this purpose. Places not to be found in the maps are referred to in the notes.

The texts of the early editions and of several later editions, English and American, have been carefully collated. It was with much hesitation that the editor ventured to make essential changes in the original punctuation, which has been followed in most of the subsequent editions that he has examined. He decided to make them, however, in the conviction that a system of punctuation more in accordance with present usage in this country would make the reading easier. A similar explanation may be made of a few changes in spelling.

A pronouncing vocabulary of proper names (according to the English method) will, it is hoped, be found useful to many readers.

The editor gratefully acknowledges his obligations to Mr. William Tappan for valuable criticisms and suggestions.

M. G. D.

January, 1899.

CONTENTS.

	PAGE
INTRODUCTION	vii
AUTHOR'S PREFACE	3
HORATIUS	27
THE BATTLE OF THE LAKE REGILLUS	53
VIRGINIA	87
THE PROPHECY OF CAPYS	109
NOTES	125
PRONOUNCING VOCABULARY	143

MAPS.

ETRURIA, LATIUM, ETC.	2
ROME UNDER THE KINGS	26

INTRODUCTION.

Thomas Babington Macaulay, son of Zachary Macaulay, an eminent philanthropist, was born Oct. 25, 1800, at Rothley Temple, Leicestershire, England. He was graduated at Trinity College, Cambridge, in 1822, and in 1824 was elected a Fellow of Trinity, remaining there till 1825. He entered Parliament in 1830. In 1834 he was made a member of the Supreme Council of India, and soon proceeded to Calcutta, where he remained till 1838. He was again elected to Parliament in 1839, appointed War-secretary in 1840, and Paymaster-general in 1846. In 1847 he was defeated in his canvass for Parliament, but was re-elected in 1852. In 1857 he was raised to the peerage of Great Britain under the title of Baron Macaulay of Rothley. He died Dec. 28, 1859, at his residence, Holly Lodge, London, and was buried in Westminster Abbey in the "Poets' Corner."

In his earliest childhood Macaulay gave evidence of the remarkable intellectual gifts with which nature had endowed him, and of his decided bent towards literary pursuits. Before he was eight years old he had written a *Compendium of Universal History* and a romance entitled *The Battle of Cheviot*. A little later he composed poems of great length. These juvenile productions are said to have been creditable performances for one of his age, or, as Hannah More said of some hymns that he had composed, "quite extraordinary for such a baby." They are mentioned here only to show how early his mental activity began to display itself.

At college he acquired a brilliant reputation as a scholar and debater, though he did not reach the highest college rank on account of his dislike of mathematical studies. He twice received the Chancellor's medal for excellence in English verse.

At the age of twenty-six he was admitted to the bar; but after a year or two he found that the law was not his vocation, and soon abandoned it altogether. Meanwhile fame was coming to him from other directions. In 1825 his first contribution to the *Edinburgh Review*, the essay on Milton, appeared, and it at once became evident that a new star had risen on the literary horizon. He continued to write for the *Review* for nearly twenty years, during which time appeared the celebrated essays on Lord Bacon, Bunyan, Lord Clive, Warren Hastings, and others, all marked by the same profundity of learning, the same wealth and aptness of illustration, the same brilliancy of fancy, the same critical acumen, and the same felicities of style that characterized his first effort.

In his political career Macaulay was an ardent Whig; but he never sacrificed his convictions of what was right to mere expediency or to popular clamor. It was his independence that cost him his seat in Parliament in 1847. In Parliament he was a skilful and ready debater, and his reputation as an exceptionally brilliant orator always attracted crowds of eager listeners whenever it was known that he was to speak.

His services in India were of great value to the government and to the people of that country. He drafted a penal code, which, after much discussion and revision, became the code under which criminal law is now administered throughout the Indian empire. He also set on foot a system of national education, which has since spread over the whole of India.

The *History of England* was to be the crowning work of

Macaulay's life, and that upon which his fame should chiefly rest. He gradually gave up all thought of further political preferment, devoting the last years of his life almost exclusively to the immense labor involved in the prosecution of this work. Unfortunately, he lived to complete only five volumes. When the first two volumes were issued, in 1848, they were received with remarkable enthusiasm on both sides of the Atlantic. In fact, no similar work had ever met with such a reception.

In the height of his fame as a statesman, orator, and writer, Macaulay achieved also great social distinction, for to his other accomplishments he added that of being a very entertaining converser and story-teller. "His family breakfast table was covered with cards of invitation to dinner from every quarter of London."

He was altogether charming in his domestic relations. He was never married, but seemed to live for his sister Hannah, to whom he was devotedly attached, and whose children he treated as his own.

No account of Macaulay, however brief, is complete without mention of his prodigious memory. He seemed to remember without effort everything that he had ever read or heard, even to the minutest details. "At one period of his life he was known to say that, if by some miracle of vandalism all copies of *Paradise Lost* and *The Pilgrim's Progress* were destroyed off the face of the earth, he would undertake to reproduce them both from recollection whenever a revival of learning came."[1] Even towards the end of his life he would sometimes devote his leisure hours to testing his memory. "I walked in the portico," he writes in October, 1857, "and learned by heart the noble Fourth Act of the *Merchant of Venice*. There are four hundred lines, of which I knew a hundred and fifty. I made myself perfect master

[1] *Life and Letters*, vol. i, p. 52.

of the whole, the prose letter included, in two hours." [1] On one occasion, in answer to a friendly challenge to a feat of memory, he drew off at once a full list of the Senior Wranglers at Cambridge, with their dates and colleges, for the hundred years during which the names of Senior Wranglers had been recorded in the University Calendar.

Through all his varied career he never ceased to keep up his acquaintance with classic literature. Even in the midst of the turmoil of political life and the incessant demands of official position, he found time to read again and again the works that most men close forever when they leave college.

In his correspondence and in his journal he makes frequent reference to this habit, as, for example: "Calcutta, Dec. 30, 1835. . . . During the last thirteen months I have read Æschylus twice; Sophocles twice; Euripides once; Pindar twice; Callimachus; Apollonius Rhodius; Quintus Calaber; Theocritus twice; Herodotus; Thucydides; almost all Xenophon's works; almost all Plato; Aristotle's Politics, and a good deal of his Organon, — besides dipping elsewhere in him; the whole of Plutarch's Lives; about half of Lucian; two or three books of Athenaeus; Plautus twice; Terence twice; Lucretius twice; Catullus; Tibullus; Propertius; Lucan; Statius; Silius Italicus; Livy; Velleius Paterculus; Sallust; Caesar; and, lastly, Cicero. [2]

Macaulay's purpose in writing the *Lays* he has fully explained in the preface. A few additional statements and remarks about them are worth quoting. Writing to the editor of the *Edinburgh Review* in July, 1842, he says: "You are acquainted, no doubt, with Perizonius's theory about the early Roman history, — a theory which Niebuhr revived, and which Arnold [3] has adopted as fully established. I have myself not the smallest doubt of its truth. It is that the

---

[1] *Life and Letters*, vol. i, p. 448.   [2] *Ibid.*, p. 443.
[3] Dr. Thomas Arnold of Rugby.

stories of the birth of Romulus and Remus, the fight of the Horatii and Curiatii, and all the other romantic tales which fill the first three or four books of Livy, came from the lost ballads of the early Romans. I amused myself in India with trying to restore some of these long-perished poems. Arnold saw two of them and wrote to me in such terms of eulogy that I have been induced to correct and complete them. There are four of them, and I think that, though they are but trifles, they may pass for scholarlike and not inelegant trifles. I must prefix short prefaces to them, and I think of publishing them next November in a small volume."[1]

The following extract from a letter to the same person, written Nov. 16, 1842, after the *Lays* had been published, shows something of his own opinion regarding them: "I am glad that you like my *Lays*, and the more glad because I know that, from good-will to me, you must have been anxious about their fate. I do not wonder at your misgivings. I should have felt similar misgivings if I had learned that any person, however distinguished by talents and knowledge, whom I knew as a writer only by prose works, was about to publish a volume of poetry. Had I seen advertised a poem by Mackintosh, by Dugald Stewart, or even by Burke, I should have augured nothing but failure; and I am far from putting myself on a level even with the least of the three. So much the better for me. Where people look for no merit, a little merit goes a long way; and, without the smallest affectation of modesty, I confess that the success of my little book has far exceeded its just claims. I shall be in no hurry to repeat the experiment; for I am well aware that a second attempt would be made under much less favorable circumstances. A far more severe test would now be applied to my verses. I shall, therefore, like a wise gamester, leave off while I am a winner, and not cry Double or Quits."[2]

[1] *Life and Letters*, vol. ii, p. 112.   [2] *Ibid*, p. 122.

In his journal, under date Sept. 9, 1850, he writes: "Those poems have now been eight years published. They still sell, and seem still to give pleasure. I do not rate them high; but I do not remember that any better poetry has been published since."[1]

The remarkable popularity of the *Lays* from the very first shows that Macaulay struck a responsive chord in the hearts of old and young alike. They were received with the warmest praise not only by the public but by the reviewers, only now and then one finding serious fault with them. Some later critics, however, have gone so far as to assert that Macaulay was no poet — that the *Lays* are not poetry; but no amount of hostile criticism, not even the great name of Matthew Arnold, seems to lessen the favor in which they are still held.

The following passages, quoted from various sources, will be of interest to the student.

"You are very right in admiring Macaulay, who has a noble, clear, metallic note in his soul, and makes us ready by it for battle. I very much admire Mr. Macaulay, and could scarcely read his ballads and keep lying down. They seemed to draw me up to my feet, as the mesmeric powers are said to do."[2]

"It is the great merit of these poems that they are free from ambition or exaggeration. Nothing seems overdone — no tawdry piece of finery disfigures the simplicity of the plan that has been chosen. They seem to have been framed with great artistical skill — with much self-denial and abstinence from anything incongruous — and with a very successful imitation of the effects intended to be represented. Set every

---

[1] *Life and Letters*, vol. ii, p. 282.
[2] *Letters of Elizabeth Barrett Browning, addressed to Richard Hengist Horne*, vol. i, p. 101.

here and there, images of beauty and expressions of feeling are thrown out that are wholly independent of Rome or the Romans, and that appeal to the widest sensibilities of the human heart. In point of homeliness of thought and language, there is often a boldness which none but a man conscious of great powers of writing would have ventured to show."[1]

" . . . the pinchbeck Roman ballads of Lord Macaulay."

"Let me frankly say that, to my mind, a man's power to detect the ring of false metal in those *Lays* is a good measure of his fitness to give an opinion about poetical matters at all."[2]

"The merits of Macaulay's poetry are similar to his prose, except that his verse is characterized by more imagination. The same living energy, however, animates both. He is a man of the most extensive acquirements, possessing the power of representing his knowledge in magnificent pictures. He has a quick sympathy with whatever addresses the passions and the fancy, and a truly masculine mind. His style alternates between copiousness and condensation, and the transitions are contrived with consummate skill. The most brilliant and rapid of all contemporary writers, his poetry is an array of strong thoughts and glittering fancies bounding along on a rushing stream of feeling. It has almost the appearance of splendid impromptu composition. The 'Lay' of 'Virginia' contains some exquisite delineations of the affections, full of natural pathos and a certain serene beauty, somewhat different from Macaulay's usual martial tone."[3]

[1] Professor Wilson, in *Blackwood's Magazine*, vol. lii, p. 802.
[2] Matthew Arnold, in *On Translating Homer*.
[3] E. P. Whipple, in *Essays and Reviews*, vol. i, p. 340 (1848).

"In them [the Roman ballads] are repeated all the merits and all the defects of the *Essays*. The men and women are mere enumerations of qualities; the battle-pieces are masses of uncombined incidents: but the characteristics of the periods treated have been caught and reproduced with perfect accuracy. The setting of Horatius, which belongs to the earliest days of Rome, is totally different from the setting of the Prophecy of Capys, which belongs to the time when Rome was fast acquiring the mastery over Italy; and in each case the setting is studiously and remarkably exact. In these poems, again, there is the same prodigious learning, the same richness of illustration, which distinguish the *Essays;* and they are adorned with a profusion of metaphor and aptness of epithets which is most admirable."[1]

"And he knows, too, how to stir the blood of the average Englishman. He understands most thoroughly the value of concentration, unity, and simplicity. Every speech or essay forms an artistic whole, in which some distinct moral is vigorously driven home by a succession of downright blows. This strong rhetorical instinct is shown conspicuously in the *Lays of Ancient Rome*, which, whatever we may say of them as poetry, are an admirable specimen of rhymed rhetoric. We know how good they are when we see how incapable are modern ballad-writers in general of putting the same swing and fire into their verses. Compare, for example, Aytoun's *Lays of the Cavaliers*, as the most obvious parallel: —

> Not swifter pours the avalanche
> Adown the steep incline,
> That rises o'er the parent springs
> Of rough and rapid Rhine,

[1] John Bach McMaster, in *Library of the World's Best Literature*, vol. xvi, p. 9384.

than certain Scotch heroes over an entrenchment. Place this mouthing by any parallel passage in Macaulay: —

> Now, by our sire Quirinus,
>   It was a goodly sight
> To see the thirty standards
>   Swept down the tide of flight.
>
> So flies the spray in Adria
>   When the black squall doth blow.
> So corn-sheaves in the flood time
>   Spin down the whirling Po.

And so on, in verses which innumerable schoolboys of inferior pretensions to Macaulay's know by heart. And in such cases the verdict of the schoolboy is perhaps more valuable than that of the literary connoisseur. There are, of course, many living poets who can do tolerably something of far higher quality which Macaulay could not do at all. But I don't know who, since Scott, could have done this particular thing. Possibly Mr. Kingsley might have approached it, or the poet, if he would have condescended so far, who sang the bearing of the good news from Ghent to Aix. In any case, the feat is significant of Macaulay's true power. It looks easy; it involves no demands upon the higher reasoning or imaginative powers: but nobody will believe it to be easy who observes the extreme rarity of a success in a feat so often attempted."[1]

"The chorus of enthusiastic applause with which the *Lays* were received — Macaulay's veteran adversary, Christopher North, shouting with the loudest, — has not, perhaps, been uniformly echoed by the critics of latter days: but with the far more important audience which lies outside the little circle of self-appointed judges and accepts their judgments

[1] Leslie Stephen, in *Hours in a Library*, vol. ii, p. 369.

only when it agrees with them, they have never lost their popularity. Every schoolboy knows them, to use a favorite phrase of Macaulay's own, though schoolboys are not usually partial to poetry; but to the minstrelsy of Scott or Macaulay — it is much to mention them together — no healthy-minded boy refuses to listen, nor should we think much of the boy who could not declaim some of the fiery sentences of Icilius, or describe exactly the manner of the death of Ocnus or Aruns, Seius or Lausulus. Of older readers it is less necessary to speak, as he who has known Macaulay's *Lays* in his childhood has no occasion to refer to them again. There is an unfading charm in the swing and vigor of the lines, which bring to our ears the very sound of the battle, the clash of steel and the rushing of the horses, 'the noise of the captains and the shouting.' 'A cut and thrust style,' Wilson called it, 'without any flourish — Scott's style when his blood was up and the first words came like a vanguard impatient for battle.' The praise is scarcely extravagant."[1]

[1] Mrs. Oliphant, in *The Victorian Age of English Literature*, vol. i, p. 174.

MACAULAY'S
LAYS OF ANCIENT ROME.

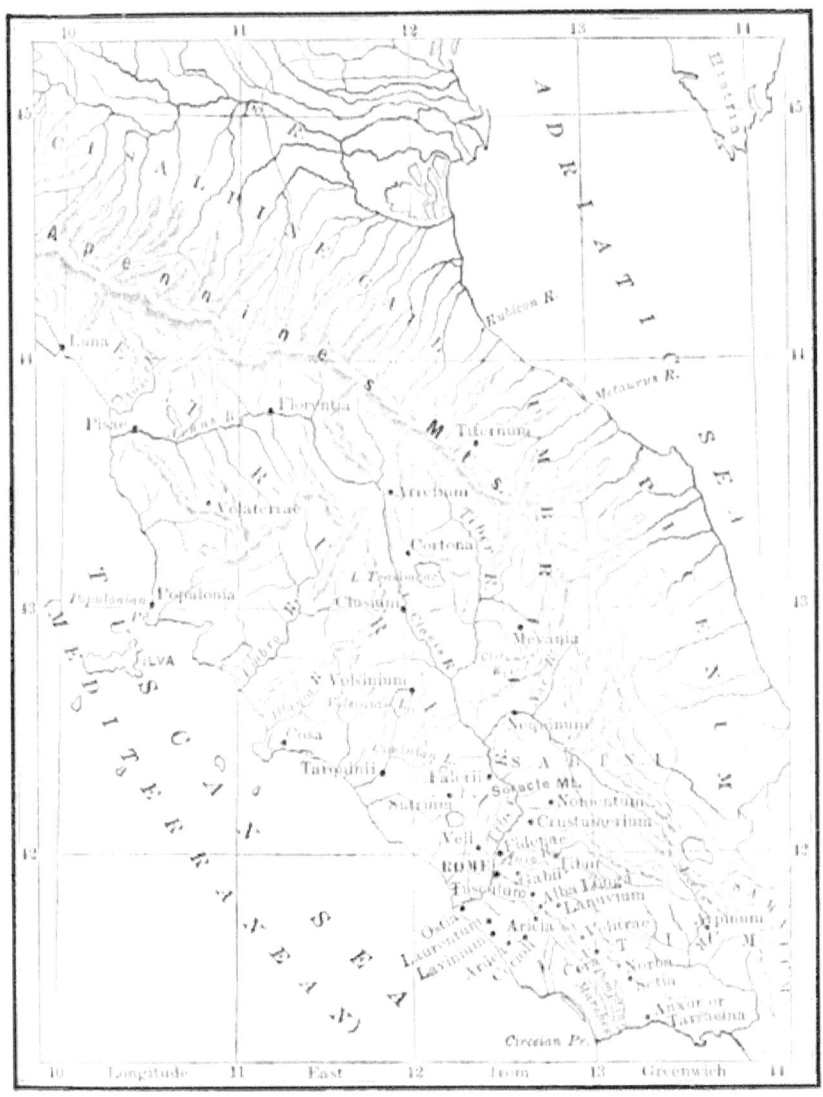

PART OF CENTRAL ITALY.

(Etruria, Latium, etc.)

LAYS OF ANCIENT ROME.

PREFACE.[1]

THAT what is called the history of the Kings and early Consuls of Rome is to a great extent fabulous, few scholars have, since the time of Beaufort, ventured to deny. It is certain that, more than three hundred and sixty years after the date ordinarily assigned for the foundation of the city, the public records were, with scarcely an exception, destroyed by the Gauls. It is certain that the oldest annals of the commonwealth were compiled more than a century and a half after this destruction of the records. It is certain, therefore, that the great Latin writers of the Augustan age did not possess those materials without which a trustworthy account of the infancy of the republic could not possibly be framed. Those writers own, indeed, that the chronicles to which they had access were filled with battles that were never fought and Consuls that were never inaugurated; and we have abundant proof that, in these chronicles, events of the greatest importance, such as the issue of the war with Porsena and the issue of the war with Brennus, were grossly misrepresented. Under these circumstances, a wise man will look with great suspicion on the legend which has come down to us. He will perhaps be inclined to regard the princes who are said to have

---

[1] This is Macaulay's general introduction to the *Lays*.

founded the civil and religious institutions of Rome, the son of Mars and the husband of Egeria, as mere mythological personages, of the same class with Perseus and Ixion. As he draws nearer and nearer to the confines of authentic history, he will become less and less hard of belief. He will admit that the most important parts of the narrative have some foundation in truth. But he will distrust almost all the details, not only because they seldom rest on any solid evidence, but also because he will constantly detect in them, even when they are within the limits of physical possibility, that peculiar character, more easily understood than defined, which distinguishes the creations of the imagination from the realities of the world in which we live.

The early history of Rome is indeed far more poetical than anything else in Latin literature. The loves of the Vestal and the God of War, the cradle laid among the reeds of Tiber, the fig-tree, the she-wolf, the shepherd's cabin, the recognition, the fratricide, the rape of the Sabines, the death of Tarpeia, the fall of Hostus Hostilius, the struggle of Mettus Curtius through the marsh, the women rushing with torn raiment and dishevelled hair between their fathers and their husbands, the nightly meetings of Numa and the Nymph by the well in the sacred grove, the fight of the three Romans and the three Albans, the purchase of the Sibylline books, the crime of Tullia, the simulated madness of Brutus, the ambiguous reply of the Delphian oracle to the Tarquins, the wrongs of Lucretia, the heroic actions of Horatius Cocles, of Scævola, and of Clœlia, the battle of Regillus won by the aid of Castor and Pollux, the defence of Cremera, the touching story of Coriolanus, the still more touching story of Virginia, the wild legend about the draining of the Alban lake, the combat between Valerius Corvus and the gigantic Gaul, are among the many instances which will at once suggest themselves to every reader.

In the narrative of Livy, who was a man of fine imagination, these stories retain much of their genuine character. Nor could even the tasteless Dionysius distort and mutilate them into mere prose. The poetry shines, in spite of him, through the dreary pedantry of his eleven books. It is discernible in the most tedious and in the most superficial modern works on the early times of Rome. It enlivens the dulness of the *Universal History*, and gives a charm to the most meagre abridgments of Goldsmith.

Even in the age of Plutarch there were discerning men who rejected the popular account of the foundation of Rome, because that account appeared to them to have the air, not of a history, but of a romance or a drama. Plutarch, who was displeased at their incredulity, had nothing better to say in reply to their arguments than that chance sometimes turns poet, and produces trains of events not to be distinguished from the most elaborate plots which are constructed by art.[1] But though the existence of a poetical element in the early history of the Great City was detected so many years ago, the first critic who distinctly saw from what source that poetical element had been derived was James Perizonius, one of the most acute and learned antiquaries of the seventeenth century. His theory, which in his own days attracted little or no

---

[1] Ὕποπτον μὲν ἐνίοις ἐστὶ τὸ δραματικὸν καὶ πλασματῶδες· οὐ δεῖ δὲ ἀπιστεῖν, τὴν τύχην ὁρῶντας, οἵων ποιημάτων δημιουργός ἐστι. — *Plut. Rom.* viii. This remarkable passage has been more grossly misinterpreted than any other in the Greek language, where the sense was so obvious. The Latin version of Cruserius, the French version of Amyot, the old English version by several hands, and the later English version by Langhorne, are all equally destitute of every trace of the meaning of the original. None of the translators saw even that ποίημα is a poem. They all render it an event.

notice, was revived in the present generation by Niebuhr, a man who would have been the first writer of his time, if his talent for communicating truths had borne any proportion to his talent for investigating them. That theory has been adopted by several eminent scholars of our own country, particularly by the Bishop of St. David's, by Professor Malden, and by the lamented Arnold. It appears to be now generally received by men conversant with classical antiquity; and indeed it rests on such strong proofs, both internal and external, that it will not be easily subverted. A popular exposition of this theory, and of the evidence by which it is supported, may not be without interest even for readers who are unacquainted with the ancient languages.

The Latin literature which has come down to us is of later date than the commencement of the Second Punic War, and consists almost exclusively of works fashioned on Greek models. The Latin metres, heroic, elegiac, lyric, and dramatic, are of Greek origin. The best Latin epic poetry is the feeble echo of the *Iliad* and *Odyssey*. The best Latin eclogues are imitations of Theocritus. The plan of the most finished didactic poem in the Latin tongue was taken from Hesiod. The Latin tragedies are bad copies of the masterpieces of Sophocles and Euripides. The Latin comedies are free translations from Demophilus, Menander, and Apollodorus. The Latin philosophy was borrowed, without alteration, from the Portico and the Academy; and the great Latin orators constantly proposed to themselves as patterns the speeches of Demosthenes and Lysias.

But there was an earlier Latin literature, a literature truly Latin, which has wholly perished, which had, indeed, almost wholly perished long before those whom we are in the habit of regarding as the greatest Latin writers were born. That literature abounded with metrical romances, such as are found in every country where there is much curiosity and intelligence, but little reading and writing. All human beings not utterly savage long for some information about past times, and are delighted by narratives which present pictures to the eye of the mind. But it is only in very enlightened communities that books are readily accessible. Metrical composition, therefore, which in a highly civilized nation is a mere luxury, is in nations imperfectly civilized almost a necessary of life, and is valued less on account of the pleasure which it gives to the ear than on account of the help which it gives to the memory. A man who can invent or embellish an interesting story, and put it into a form which others may easily retain in their recollection, will always be highly esteemed by a people eager for amusement and information, but destitute of libraries. Such is the origin of ballad-poetry, a species of composition which scarcely ever fails to spring up and flourish in every society at a certain point in the progress towards refinement. Tacitus informs us that songs were the only memorials of the past which the ancient Germans possessed. We learn from Lucan and from Ammianus Marcellinus that the brave actions of the ancient Gauls were commemorated in the verses of Bards. During many ages, and through many revolutions, minstrelsy retained its influence over both the Teutonic and the Celtic race. The vengeance exacted by the spouse of Attila for the murder of Siegfried was celebrated in rhymes, of which Germany is still justly proud. The exploits of Athelstane were commemorated by the Anglo-Saxons, and those of Canute by the Danes, in rude poems, of which a few fragments have come down to us. The chants of the Welsh harpers preserved, through ages of darkness, a faint and doubtful memory of Arthur. In the Highlands of Scotland may still be gleaned some relics of the old songs about Cuthullin and Fingal. The long struggle of the Servians against the Ottoman power was recorded in lays full of martial spirit. We learn from Herrera that, when a Peruvian Inca died, men of skill were appointed to celebrate him in verses, which all the people learned by heart and sang in public on days of festival. The feats of Kurroglou, the great freebooter of Turkistan, recounted in ballads composed by himself, are known in every village of Northern Persia. Captain Beechey heard the Bards of the Sandwich Islands recite the heroic achievements of Tamehameha, the most illustrious of their kings. Mungo Park found in the heart of Africa a class of singing-men, the only annalists of their rude tribes, and heard them tell the story of the victory which Damel, the negro prince of the Jaloffs, won over Abdulkader, the Mussulman tyrant of Foota Torra. This species of poetry attained a high degree of excellence among the Castilians before they began to copy Tuscan patterns. It attained a still higher degree of excellence among the English and the Lowland Scotch during the fourteenth, fifteenth, and sixteenth centuries. But it reached its full perfection in ancient Greece; for there can be no doubt that the great Homeric poems are generically ballads, though widely distinguished from all other ballads, and indeed from almost all other human compositions, by transcendent sublimity and beauty.

As it is agreeable to general experience that, at a certain stage in the progress of society, ballad-poetry should flourish, so is it also agreeable to general experience that, at a subsequent stage in the progress of society, ballad-poetry should be undervalued and neglected. Knowledge advances; manners change; great foreign models of composition are studied and imitated. The phraseology of the old minstrels becomes obsolete. Their versification, which, having received its laws only from the ear, abounds in irregularities, seems licentious and uncouth. Their simplicity appears beggarly when compared with the quaint forms and gaudy coloring of such artists as Cowley and Gongora. The ancient lays, unjustly despised by the learned and polite, linger for a time in the memory of the vulgar, and are at length too often irretrievably lost. We cannot wonder that the ballads of Rome should have altogether disappeared, when we remember how very narrowly, in spite of the invention of printing, those of our own country and those of Spain escaped the same fate. There is indeed little doubt that oblivion covers many English songs equal to any that were published by Bishop Percy, and many Spanish songs as good as the best of those which have been so happily translated by Mr. Lockhart. Eighty years ago England possessed only one tattered copy of *Childe Waters* and *Sir Cauline*, and Spain only one tattered copy of the noble poem of *The Cid*. The snuff of a candle, or a mischievous dog, might in a moment have deprived the world forever of any of those fine compositions. Sir Walter Scott, who united to the fire of a great poet the minute curiosity and patient diligence of a great antiquary, was but just in time to save the precious relics of the Minstrelsy of the Border. In Germany, the lay of the Nibelungs had been long utterly forgotten, when, in the eighteenth century, it was for the first time printed from a manuscript in the old library of a noble family. In truth, the only people who, through their whole passage from simplicity to the highest civilization, never for a moment ceased to love and admire their old ballads, were the Greeks.

That the early Romans should have had ballad-poetry, and that this poetry should have perished, is therefore not strange. It would, on the contrary, have been strange if these things had not come to pass; and we should be justified in pronouncing them highly probable, even if we had no direct evidence on the subject. But we have direct evidence of unquestionable authority.

Ennius, who flourished in the time of the Second Punic War, was regarded in the Augustan age as the father of Latin poetry. He was, in truth, the father of the second school of Latin poetry, the only school of which the works have descended to us. But from Ennius himself we learn that there were poets who stood to him in the same relation in which the author of the romance of *Count Alarcos* stood to Garcilaso, or the author of the *Lytell Geste of Robyn Hode* to Lord Surrey. Ennius speaks of verses which the Fauns and the Bards were wont to chant in the old time, when none had yet studied the graces of speech, when none had yet climbed the peaks sacred to the Goddesses of Grecian song. "Where," Cicero mournfully asks, "are those old verses now?"[1]

[1] 'Quid? Nostri veteres versus ubi sunt?
. . . "Quos olim Fauni vatesque canebant
Cum neque Musarum scopulos quisquam superârat,
Nec dicti studiosus erat."' *Brutus*, xviii.

The Muses, it should be observed, are Greek divinities. The Italian Goddesses of verse were the Camœnæ. At a later period the appellations were used indiscriminately; but in the age of Ennius there was probably a distinction. In the epitaph of Nævius, who was the representative of the old Italian school of poetry, the Camœnæ, not the Muses, are represented as grieving for the loss of their votary. The 'Musarum scopuli' are evidently the peaks of Parnassus.

Scaliger, in a note on Varro (*De Lingua Latina*, lib. vi.), suggests, with great ingenuity, that the Fauns, who were represented by the superstition of later ages as a race of monsters, half gods and half brutes, may really have been a class of men who exercised in Latium, at a very remote period, the same functions which belonged to the Magians in Persia and to the Bards in Gaul.

Contemporary with Ennius was Quintus Fabius Pictor, the earliest of the Roman annalists. His account of the infancy and youth of Romulus and Remus has been preserved by Dionysius, and contains a very remarkable reference to the ancient Latin poetry. Fabius says that, in his time, his countrymen were still in the habit of singing ballads about the Twins. "Even in the hut of Faustulus," — so these old lays appear to have run, — "the children of Rhea and Mars were, in port and in spirit, not like unto swineherds or cowherds, but such that men might well guess them to be of the blood of Kings and Gods."[1]

[1] Οἱ δὲ ἀνδρωθέντες γίνονται, κατά τε ἀξίωσιν μορφῆς καὶ φρονήματος ὄγκον, οὐ συοφορβοῖς καὶ βουκόλοις ἐοικότες, ἀλλ' οἵους ἄν τις ἀξιώσειε τοὺς ἐκ βασιλείου τε φύντας γένους, καὶ ἀπὸ δαιμόνων σπορᾶς γενέσθαι νομιζομένους, ὡς ἐν τοῖς πατρίοις ὕμνοις ὑπὸ ʽΡωμαίων ἔτι καὶ νῦν ᾄδεται. — Dion. Hal. i. 79. This passage has sometimes been cited as if Dionysius had been speaking in his own person, and had, Greek as he was, been so industrious or so fortunate as to discover some valuable remains of that early Latin poetry which the greatest Latin writers of his age regretted as hopelessly lost. Such a supposition is highly improbable; and indeed it seems clear from the context that Dionysius, as Reiske and other editors evidently thought, was merely quoting from Fabius Pictor. The whole passage has the air of an extract from an ancient chronicle, and is introduced by the words, Κόϊντος μὲν Φάβιος, ὁ Πίκτωρ λεγόμενος, τῇδε γράφει.

Another argument may be urged which seems to deserve consideration. The author of the passage in question mentions a thatched hut, which in his time stood between the summit of Mount Palatine and the Circus. This hut, he says, was built by Romulus, and was constantly kept in repair at the public charge, but never in any respect embellished. Now, in the age of Dionysius there certainly was at Rome a thatched hut, said to have been that of Romulus. But this hut, as we learn from Vitruvius, stood, not near the Circus, but in the Capitol (Vit. ii. 1). If, therefore, we understand Dionysius to speak in his own person, we can reconcile his statement with that of Vitruvius only by supposing that there were at Rome, in the Augustan age, two thatched huts, both believed to have been built by Romulus, and both carefully repaired and held

Cato the Censor, who also lived in the days of the Second Punic War, mentioned this lost literature in his lost work on the antiquities of his country. Many ages, he said, before his time, there were ballads in praise of illustrious men; and these ballads it was the fashion for the

in high honor. The objections to such a supposition seem to be strong. Neither Dionysius nor Vitruvius speaks of more than one such hut. Dio Cassius informs us that twice, during the long administration of Augustus, the hut of Romulus caught fire (xlviii. 43, liv. 29). Had there been two such huts, would he not have told us of which he spoke? An English historian would hardly give an account of a fire at Queen's College without saying whether it was at Queen's College, Oxford, or at Queen's College, Cambridge. Marcus Seneca, Macrobius, and Conon, a Greek writer from whom Photius has made large extracts, mention only one hut of Romulus, that in the Capitol (M. Seneca, *Contr.* i. 6; Macrobius, *Sat.* i. 15; Photius, *Bibl.* 186). Ovid, Livy, Petronius, Valerius Maximus, Lucius Seneca, and St. Jerome mention only one hut of Romulus, without specifying the site (Ovid, *Fasti*, iii. 183; Liv. v. 53; Petronius, *Fragm.*; Val. Max. iv. 4; L. Seneca, *Consolatio ad Helviam*; D. Hieron. *Ad Paulinianum de Didymo*).

The whole difficulty is removed if we suppose that Dionysius was merely quoting Fabius Pictor. Nothing is more probable than that the cabin, which in the time of Fabius stood near the Circus, might, long before the age of Augustus, have been transported to the Capitol, as the place fittest, by reason both of its safety and of its sanctity, to contain so precious a relic.

The language of Plutarch confirms this hypothesis. He describes with great precision the spot where Romulus dwelt, on the slope of Mount Palatine leading to the Circus; but he says not a word implying that the dwelling was still to be seen there. Indeed, his expressions imply that it was no longer there. The evidence of Solinus is still more to the point. He, like Plutarch, describes the spot where Romulus had resided, and says expressly that the hut had been there, but that in his time it was there no longer. The site, it is certain, was well remembered; and probably retained its old name, as Charing Cross and the Haymarket have done. This is probably the explanation of the words 'Casa Romuli' in Victor's description of the Tenth Region of Rome under Valentinian.

guests at banquets to sing in turn while the piper played. "Would," exclaims Cicero, "that we still had the old ballads of which Cato speaks!"[1]

Valerius Maximus gives us exactly similar information, without mentioning his authority, and observes that the ancient Roman ballads were probably of more benefit to the young than all the lectures of the Athenian schools, and that to the influence of the national poetry were to be ascribed the virtues of such men as Camillus and Fabricius.[2]

Varro, whose authority on all questions connected with the antiquities of his country is entitled to the greatest respect, tells us that at banquets it was once the fashion for boys to sing, sometimes with and sometimes without instrumental music, ancient ballads in praise of men of former times. These young performers, he observes, were of unblemished character, a circumstance which he probably mentioned because among the Greeks, and indeed in his time among the Romans also, the morals of singing-boys were in no high repute.[3]

---

[1] Cicero refers twice to this important passage in Cato's *Antiquities:* 'Gravissimus auctor in Originibus dixit Cato, morem apud majores hunc epularum fuisse, ut deinceps, qui accubarent, canerent ad tibiam clarorum virorum laudes atque virtutes. Ex quo perspicuum est, et cantus tum fuisse rescriptos vocum sonis, et carmina.' — *Tusc. Quæst.* iv. 2. Again : 'Utinam exstarent illa carmina, quæ, multis sæculis ante suam ætatem, in epulis esse cantitata a singulis convivis de clarorum virorum laudibus, in Originibus scriptum reliquit Cato.' — *Brutus*, xix.

[2] 'Majores natu in conviviis ad tibias egregia superiorum opera carmine comprehensa pangebant, quo ad ea imitanda juventutem alacriorem redderent.... Quas Athenas, quam scholam, quæ alienigena studia huic domesticæ disciplinæ prætulerim? Inde oriebantur Camilli, Scipiones, Fabricii, Marcelli, Fabii.' — Val. Max. ii. 1.

[3] 'In conviviis pueri modesti ut cantarent carmina antiqua, in quibus laudes erant majorum, et assa voce, et cum tibicine.' — Nonius, *Assa voce pro sola.*

The testimony of Horace, though given incidentally, confirms the statements of Cato, Valerius Maximus, and Varro. The poet predicts that, under the peaceful administration of Augustus, the Romans will, over their full goblets, sing to the pipe, after the fashion of their fathers, the deeds of brave captains, and the ancient legends touching the origin of the city.[1]

The proposition, then, that Rome had ballad-poetry is not merely in itself highly probable, but is fully proved by direct evidence of the greatest weight.

This proposition being established, it becomes easy to understand why the early history of the city is unlike almost everything else in Latin literature, native where almost everything else is borrowed, imaginative where almost everything else is prosaic. We can scarcely hesitate to pronounce that the magnificent, pathetic, and truly national legends, which present so striking a contrast to all that surrounds them, are broken and defaced fragments of that early poetry which, even in the age of Cato the Censor, had become antiquated, and of which Tully had never heard a line.

That this poetry should have been suffered to perish will not appear strange when we consider how complete was the triumph of the Greek genius over the public mind of Italy. It is probable that at an early period Homer and Herodotus furnished some hints to the Latin min-

---

[1] 'Nosque et profestis lucibus et sacris
  Inter jocosi munera Liberi,
    Cum prole matronisque nostris,
      Rite Deos prius apprecati,
    Virtute functos, more patrum, duces,
  Lydis remixto carmine tibiis,
    Trojamque et Anchisen et almæ
      Progeniem Veneris canemus.'

Carm. iv. 15.

strels;[1] but it was not till after the war with Pyrrhus that
the poetry of Rome began to put off its old Ausonian
character. The transformation was soon consummated.
The conquered, says Horace, led captive the conquerors.
It was precisely at the time at which the Roman people
rose to unrivalled political ascendancy that they stooped to
pass under the intellectual yoke. It was precisely at the
time at which the sceptre departed from Greece that the
empire of her language and of her arts became universal
and despotic. The revolution indeed was not effected
without a struggle. Nævius seems to have been the last
of the ancient line of poets. Ennius was the founder
of a new dynasty. Nævius celebrated the First Punic
War in Saturnian verse, the old national verse of Italy.[2]

---

[1] See the Preface to the *Lay of the Battle of Regillus*.

[2] Cicero speaks highly in more than one place of this poem of
Nævius; Ennius sneered at it, and stole from it.

As to the Saturnian measure, see Hermann's *Elementa Doctrinæ
Metricæ*, iii. 9.

The Saturnian line, according to the grammarians, consisted of
two parts. The first was a catalectic dimeter iambic; the second
was composed of three trochees. But the license taken by the early
Latin poets seems to have been almost boundless. The most perfect Saturnian line which has been preserved was the work, not of a
professional artist, but of an amateur:

'Dabunt malum Metelli Nævio poetæ.'

There has been much difference of opinion among learned men
respecting the history of this measure. That it is the same with
a Greek measure used by Archilochus is indisputable. (Bentley,
Phalaris, xi.) But in spite of the authority of Terentianus Maurus,
and of the still higher authority of Bentley, we may venture to doubt
whether the coincidence was not fortuitous. We constantly find
the same rude and simple numbers in different countries, under circumstances which make it impossible to suspect that there has been
imitation on either side. Bishop Heber heard the children of a village in Bengal singing 'Radha, Radha,' to the tune of 'My boy Billy.'

Ennius sang the Second Punic War in numbers borrowed from the *Iliad*. The elder poet, in the epitaph which he wrote for himself, and which is a fine specimen of the early Roman diction and versification, plaintively boasted

Neither the Castilian nor the German minstrels of the Middle Ages owed anything to Paros or to ancient Rome. Yet both the poem of the Cid and the poem of the Nibelungs contain many Saturnian verses; as —

> 'Estas nuevas á mio Cid eran venidas.'
> 'Á mi lo dicen; á ti dan las orejades.'

> 'Man möhte michel wunder von Sifride sagen.'
> 'Wa ich den Künic vinde daz sol man mir sagen.'

Indeed there cannot be a more perfect Saturnian line than one which is sung in every English nursery —

> 'The queen was in her parlor eating bread and honey;'

yet the author of this line, we may be assured, borrowed nothing from either Nævius or Archilochus.

On the other hand, it is by no means improbable that, two or three hundred years before the time of Ennius, some Latin minstrel may have visited Sybaris or Crotona, may have heard some verses of Archilochus sung, may have been pleased with the metre, and may have introduced it at Rome. Thus much is certain, that the Saturnian measure, if not a native of Italy, was at least so early and so completely naturalized there that its foreign origin was forgotten.

Bentley says, indeed, that the Saturnian measure was first brought from Greece into Italy by Nævius. But this is merely *obiter dictum*, to use a phrase common in our courts of law, and would not have been deliberately maintained by that incomparable critic, whose memory is held in reverence by all lovers of learning. The arguments which might be brought against Bentley's assertion — for it is mere assertion, supported by no evidence — are innumerable. A few will suffice.

1. Bentley's assertion is opposed to the testimony of Ennius. Ennius sneered at Nævius for writing on the First Punic War in verses such as the old Italian bards used before Greek literature had been studied. Now the poem of Nævius was in Saturnian

that the Latin language had died with him.[1] Thus what to Horace appeared to be the first faint dawn of Roman literature, appeared to Nævius to be its hopeless setting. In truth, one literature was setting and another dawning.

The victory of the foreign taste was decisive; and indeed we can hardly blame the Romans for turning away with contempt from the rude lays which had delighted their fathers, and giving their whole admiration to the immortal productions of Greece. The national romances, neglected by the great and the refined whose education had been finished at Rhodes or Athens, continued, it may be sup-

---

verse. Is it possible that Ennius could have used such expressions if the Saturnian verse had been just imported from Greece for the first time?

2. Bentley's assertion is opposed to the testimony of Horace. 'When Greece,' says Horace, 'introduced her arts into our uncivilized country, those rugged Saturnian numbers passed away.' Would Horace have said this if the Saturnian numbers had been imported from Greece just before the hexameter?

3. Bentley's assertion is opposed to the testimony of Festus and of Aurelius Victor, both of whom positively say that the most ancient prophecies attributed to the Fauns were in Saturnian verse.

4. Bentley's assertion is opposed to the testimony of Terentianus Maurus, to whom he has himself appealed. Terentianus Maurus does indeed say that the Saturnian measure, though believed by the Romans from a very early period ('credidit vetustas') to be of Italian invention, was really borrowed from the Greeks. But Terentianus Maurus does not say that it was first borrowed by Nævius. Nay, the expressions used by Terentianus Maurus clearly imply the contrary; for how could the Romans have believed, from a very early period, that this measure was the indigenous production of Latium, if it was really brought over from Greece in an age of intelligence and liberal curiosity, in the age which gave birth to Ennius, Plautus, Cato the Censor, and other distinguished writers? If Bentley's assertion were correct, there could have been no more doubt at Rome about the Greek origin of the Saturnian measure than about the Greek origin of hexameters or Sapphics.

[1] Aulus Gellius, *Noctes Atticæ*, i. 24.

posed, during some generations to delight the vulgar. While Virgil, in hexameters of exquisite modulation, described the sports of rustics, those rustics were still singing their wild Saturnian ballads.[1] It is not improbable that, at the time when Cicero lamented the irreparable loss of the poems mentioned by Cato, a search among the nooks of the Apennines as active as the search which Sir Walter Scott made among the descendants of the mosstroopers of Liddesdale might have brought to light many fine remains of ancient minstrelsy. No such search was made. The Latin ballads perished forever. Yet discerning critics have thought that they could still perceive in the early history of Rome numerous fragments of this lost poetry, as the traveller on classic ground sometimes finds, built into the heavy wall of a fort or convent, a pillar rich with acanthus leaves, or a frieze where the Amazons and Bacchanals seem to live. The theatres and temples of the Greek and the Roman were degraded into the quarries of the Turk and the Goth. Even so did the ancient Saturnian poetry become the quarry in which a crowd of orators and annalists found the materials for their prose.

It is not difficult to trace the process by which the old songs were transmuted into the form which they now wear. Funeral panegyric and chronicle appear to have been the intermediate links which connected the lost ballads with the histories now extant. From a very early period it was the usage that an oration should be pronounced over the remains of a noble Roman. The orator, as we learn from Polybius, was expected on such an occasion to recapitulate all the services which the ancestors of the deceased had, from the earliest time, rendered to the commonwealth. There can be little doubt that the speaker on whom this duty was imposed would make use of all the

---

[1] See Servius, *in Georg.* ii. 385.

stories suited to his purpose which were to be found in the popular lays. There can be as little doubt that the family of an eminent man would preserve a copy of the speech which had been pronounced over his corpse. The compilers of the early chronicles would have recourse to these speeches; and the great historians of a later period would have recourse to the chronicles.

It may be worth while to select a particular story, and to trace its probable progress through these stages. The description of the migration of the Fabian house to Cremera is one of the finest of the many fine passages which lie thick in the earlier books of Livy. The Consul, clad in his military garb, stands in the vestibule of his house, marshalling his clan, three hundred and six fighting men, all of the same proud patrician blood, all worthy to be attended by the fasces and to command the legions. A sad and anxious retinue of friends accompanies the adventurers through the streets; but the voice of lamentation is drowned by the shouts of admiring thousands.

As the procession passes the Capitol, prayers and vows are poured forth, but in vain. The devoted band, leaving Janus on the right, marches to its doom through the Gate of Evil Luck. After achieving high deeds of valor against overwhelming numbers, all perish save one child, the stock from which the great Fabian race was destined again to spring for the safety and glory of the commonwealth. That this fine romance, the details of which are so full of poetical truth, and so utterly destitute of all show of historical truth, came originally from some lay which had often been sung with great applause at banquets, is in the highest degree probable. Nor is it difficult to imagine a mode in which the transmission might have taken place.

The celebrated Quintus Fabius Maximus, who died about twenty years before the First Punic War, and more than forty years before Ennius was born, is said to have been interred with extraordinary pomp. In the eulogy pronounced over his body all the great exploits of his ancestors were doubtless recounted and exaggerated. If there were then extant songs which gave a vivid and touching description of an event, the saddest and the most glorious in the long history of the Fabian house, nothing could be more natural than that the panegyrist should borrow from such songs their finest touches, in order to adorn his speech. A few generations later the songs would perhaps be forgotten, or remembered only by shepherds and vine-dressers. But the speech would certainly be preserved in the archives of the Fabian nobles. Fabius Pictor would be well acquainted with a document so interesting to his personal feelings, and would insert large extracts from it in his rude chronicle. That chronicle, as we know, was the oldest to which Livy had access. Livy would at a glance distinguish the bold strokes of the forgotten poet from the dull and feeble narrative by which they were surrounded, would retouch them with a delicate and powerful pencil, and would make them immortal.

That this might happen at Rome can scarcely be doubted; for something very like this has happened in several countries, and, among others, in our own. Perhaps the theory of Perizonius cannot be better illustrated than by showing that what he supposes to have taken place in ancient times has, beyond all doubt, taken place in modern times.

"History," says Hume with the utmost gravity, "has preserved some instances of Edgar's amours, from which, as from a specimen, we may form a conjecture of the rest." He then tells very agreeably the stories of Elfleda and Elfrida, two stories which have a most suspicious air of romance, and which indeed greatly resemble, in their general character, some of the legends of early Rome. He cites, as his authority for these two tales, the chronicle of William of Malmesbury, who lived in the time of King Stephen. The great majority of readers suppose that the device by which Elfrida was substituted for her young mistress, the artifice by which Athelwold obtained the hand of Elfrida, the detection of that artifice, the hunting party, and the vengeance of the amorous king, are things about which there is no more doubt than about the execution of Anne Boleyn or the slitting of Sir John Coventry's nose. But when we turn to William of Malmesbury, we find that Hume, in his eagerness to relate these pleasant fables, has overlooked one very important circumstance. William does indeed tell both the stories; but he gives us distinct notice that he does not warrant their truth, and that they rest on no better authority than that of ballads.[1]

Such is the way in which these two well-known tales have been handed down. They originally appeared in a poetical form. They found their way from ballads into an old chronicle. The ballads perished; the chronicle remained. A great historian, some centuries after the ballads had been altogether forgotten, consulted the chronicle. He was struck by the lively coloring of these ancient fictions; he transferred them to his pages; and thus we find inserted, as unquestionable facts, in a narrative which is likely to last as long as the English tongue, the inventions of some minstrel whose works were probably never committed to writing, whose name is buried in oblivion, and whose dialect has become obsolete. It

---

[1] 'Infamias quas post dicam magis resperserunt cantilenæ.' Edgar appears to have been most mercilessly treated in the Anglo-Saxon ballads. He was the favorite of the monks; and the monks and the minstrels were at deadly feud.

must, then, be admitted to be possible, or rather highly probable, that the stories of Romulus and Remus, and of the Horatii and Curiatii, may have had a similar origin.

Castilian literature will furnish us with another parallel case. Mariana, the classical historian of Spain, tells the story of the ill-starred marriage which the King Don Alonzo brought about between the heirs of Carrion and the two daughters of the Cid. The Cid bestowed a princely dower on his sons-in-law. But the young men were base and proud, cowardly and cruel. They were tried in danger, and found wanting. They fled before the Moors, and once, when a lion broke out of his den, they ran and crouched in an unseemly hiding-place. They knew that they were despised, and took counsel how they might be avenged. They parted from their father-in-law with many signs of love, and set forth on a journey with Doña Elvira and Doña Sol. In a solitary place the bridegrooms seized their brides, stripped them, scourged them, and departed, leaving them for dead. But one of the house of Bivar, suspecting foul play, had followed the travellers in disguise. The ladies were brought back safe to the house of their father. Complaint was made to the king. It was adjudged by the Cortes that the dower given by the Cid should be returned, and that the heirs of Carrion, together with one of their kindred, should do battle against three knights of the party of the Cid. The guilty youths would have declined the combat; but all their shifts were vain. They were vanquished in the lists and forever disgraced, while their injured wives were sought in marriage by great princes.[1]

Some Spanish writers have labored to show, by an examination of dates and circumstances, that this story is untrue. Such confutation was surely not needed; for

---

[1] Mariana, lib. x. cap. 4.

the narrative is on the face of it a romance. How it found its way into Mariana's history is quite clear. He acknowledges his obligations to the ancient chronicles, and had doubtless before him the *Cronica del famoso Cavallero Cid Ruy Diez Campeador*, which had been printed as early as the year 1552. He little suspected that all the most striking passages in this chronicle were copied from a poem of the twelfth century, a poem of which the language and versification had long been obsolete, but which glowed with no common portion of the fire of the *Iliad*. Yet such was the fact. More than a century and a half after the death of Mariana, this venerable ballad, of which one imperfect copy on parchment, four hundred years old, had been preserved at Bivar, was for the first time printed. Then it was found that every interesting circumstance of the story of the heirs of Carrion was derived by the eloquent Jesuit from a song of which he had never heard, and which was composed by a minstrel whose very name had long been forgotten.[1]

Such, or nearly such, appears to have been the process by which the lost ballad-poetry of Rome was transformed into history. To reverse that process, to transform some portions of early Roman history back into the poetry out of which they were made, is the object of this work.

In the following poems the author speaks, not in his own person, but in the persons of ancient minstrels who know only what a Roman citizen, born three or four hundred years before the Christian era, may be supposed to have known, and who are in nowise above the passions

---

[1] See the account which Sanchez gives of the Bivar manuscript in the first volume of the *Coleccion de Poesias Castellanas anteriores al Siglo XV*. Part of the story of the lords of Carrion, in the poem of the Cid, has been translated by Mr. Frere in a manner above all praise.

and prejudices of their age and nation. To these imaginary poets must be ascribed some blunders which are so obvious that it is unnecessary to point them out. The real blunder would have been to represent these old poets as deeply versed in general history and studious of chronological accuracy. To them must also be attributed the illiberal sneers at the Greeks, the furious party-spirit, the contempt for the arts of peace, the love of war for its own sake, the ungenerous exultation over the vanquished, which the reader will sometimes observe. To portray a Roman of the age of Camillus or Curius as superior to national antipathies, as mourning over the devastation and slaughter by which empire and triumphs were to be won, as looking on human suffering with the sympathy of Howard, or as treating conquered enemies with the delicacy of the Black Prince, would be to violate all dramatic propriety. The old Romans had some great virtues, — fortitude, temperance, veracity, spirit to resist oppression, respect for legitimate authority, fidelity in the observing of contracts, disinterestedness, ardent patriotism; but Christian charity and chivalrous generosity were alike unknown to them.

It would have been obviously improper to mimic the manner of any particular age or country. Something has been borrowed, however, from our own old ballads, and more from Sir Walter Scott, the great restorer of our ballad-poetry. To the *Iliad* still greater obligations are due; and those obligations have been contracted with the less hesitation, because there is reason to believe that some of the old Latin minstrels really had recourse to that inexhaustible store of poetical images.

It would have been easy to swell this little volume to a very considerable bulk by appending notes filled with quotations; but to a learned reader such notes are not necessary; for an unlearned reader they would have little interest; and the judgment passed both by the learned and by the unlearned on a work of the imagination will always depend much more on the general character and spirit of such a work than on minute details.

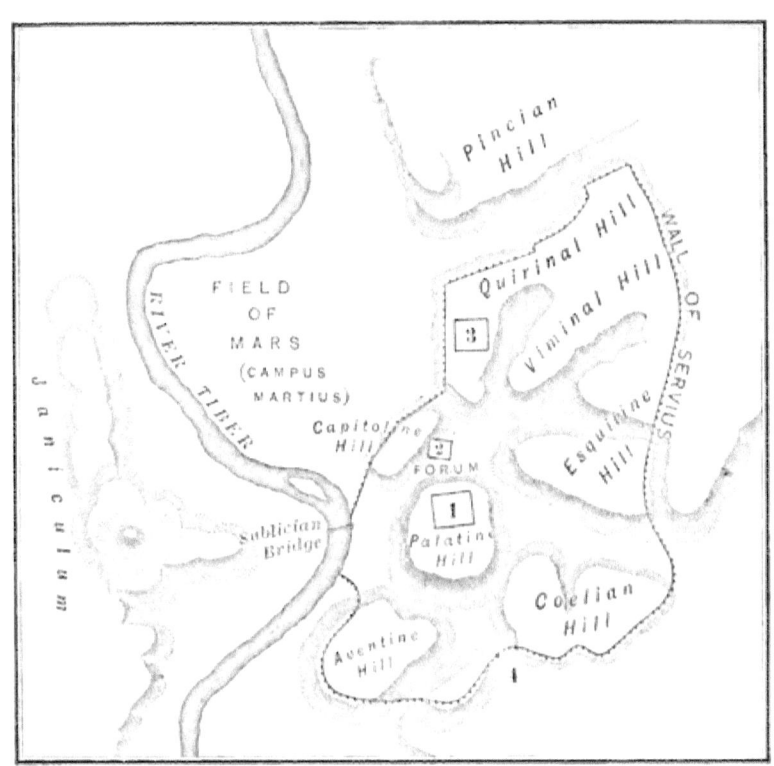

ROME UNDER THE KINGS.

1. "Square Rome" (*Roma Quadrata*), the city of Romulus.
2. The Comitium.
3. The Sabine City.
4. The Latin Gate.

HORATIUS.

THERE can be little doubt that among those parts of early Roman history which had a poetical origin was the legend of Horatius Cocles. We have several versions of the story, and these versions differ from each other in points of no small importance. Polybius, there is reason to believe, heard the tale recited over the remains of some Consul or Prætor descended from the old Horatian patricians; for he introduces it as a specimen of the narratives with which the Romans were in the habit of embellishing their funeral oratory. It is remarkable that, according to him, Horatius defended the bridge alone, and perished in the waters. According to the chronicles which Livy and Dionysius followed, Horatius had two companions, swam safe to shore, and was loaded with honors and rewards.

These discrepancies are easily explained. Our own literature, indeed, will furnish an exact parallel to what may have taken place at Rome. It is highly probable that the memory of the war of Porsena was preserved by compositions much resembling the two ballads which stand first in the *Relics of Ancient English Poetry*. In both those ballads the English, commanded by the Percy, fight with the Scots, commanded by the Douglas. In one of the ballads the Douglas is killed by a nameless English archer, and the Percy by a Scottish spearman; in the other the Percy slays the Douglas in single combat, and is himself made prisoner. In the former Sir

Hugh Montgomery is shot through the heart by a Northumbrian bowman; in the latter he is taken, and exchanged for the Percy. Yet both the ballads relate to the same event, and that an event which probably took place within the memory of persons who were alive when both the ballads were made. One of the minstrels says:

> "Old men that knowen the grounde well yenoughe
> Call it the battell of Otterburn:
> At Otterburn began this spurne
> Upon a monnyn day.
> Ther was the dougghte Doglas slean:
> The Perse never went away."

The other poet sums up the event in the following lines:

> "Thys fraye bygan at Otterborne
> Bytwene the nyghte and the day:
> Ther the Dowglas lost hys lyfe,
> And the Percy was lede away."

It is by no means unlikely that there were two old Roman lays about the defence of the bridge; and that, while the story which Livy has transmitted to us was preferred by the multitude, the other, which ascribed the whole glory to Horatius alone, may have been the favorite with the Horatian house.

The following ballad is supposed to have been made about a hundred and twenty years after the war which it celebrates, and just before the taking of Rome by the Gauls. The author seems to have been an honest citizen, proud of the military glory of his country, sick of the disputes of factions, and much given to pining after good old times which had never really existed. The allusion, however, to the partial manner in which the public lands were allotted, could proceed only from a plebeian; and the allusion to the fraudulent sale of spoils marks the date of the poem, and shows that the poet shared in the general discontent with which the proceedings of Camillus, after the taking of Veii, were regarded.

The penultimate syllable of the name Porsena has been shortened in spite of the authority of Niebuhr, who pronounces, without assigning any ground for his opinion, that Martial was guilty of a decided blunder in the line,

"Hanc spectare manum Porsena non potuit."

It is not easy to understand how any modern scholar, whatever his attainments may be, — and those of Niebuhr were undoubtedly immense, — can venture to pronounce that Martial did not know the quantity of a word which he must have uttered and heard uttered a hundred times before he left school. Niebuhr seems also to have forgotten that Martial has fellow-culprits to keep him in countenance. Horace has committed the same decided blunder; for he gives us, as a pure iambic line,

"Minacis aut Etrusca Porsenae manus."

Silius Italicus has repeatedly offended in the same way, as when he says,

"Cernitur effugiens ardentem Porsena dextram:"

and again,

"Clusinum vulgus, cum, Porsena magne, jubebas."

A modern writer may be content to err in such company.

Niebuhr's supposition, that each of the three defenders of the bridge was the representative of one of the three patrician tribes, is both ingenious and probable, and has been adopted in the following poem.

HORATIUS.

A LAY MADE ABOUT THE YEAR OF THE CITY CCCLX.

I.

Lars Porsena of Clusium
   By the Nine Gods he swore
That the great house of Tarquin
   Should suffer wrong no more.
By the Nine Gods he swore it,
   And named a trysting day,
And bade his messengers ride forth,
East and west and south and north,
   To summon his array.

II.

East and west and south and north
   The messengers ride fast,
And tower and town and cottage
   Have heard the trumpet's blast.
Shame on the false Etruscan
   Who lingers in his home,
When Porsena of Clusium
   Is on the march for Rome!

III.

The horsemen and the footmen
   Are pouring in amain
From many a stately market-place,
   From many a fruitful plain;
From many a lonely hamlet,
   Which, hid by beech and pine,

Like an eagle's nest, hangs on the crest
   Of purple Apennine ;   25

IV.

From lordly Volaterræ,
   Where scowls the far-famed hold
Piled by the hands of giants
   For godlike kings of old ;
From sea-girt Populonia,   30
   Whose sentinels descry
Sardinia's snowy mountain-tops
   Fringing the southern sky ;

V.

From the proud mart of Pisæ,
   Queen of the western waves,   35
Where ride Massilia's triremes
   Heavy with fair-haired slaves ;
From where sweet Clanis wanders
   Through corn and vines and flowers;
From where Cortona lifts to heaven   40
   Her diadem of towers.

VI.

Tall are the oaks whose acorns
   Drop in dark Auser's rill ;
Fat are the stags that champ the boughs
   Of the Ciminian hill ;   45
Beyond all streams Clitumnus
   Is to the herdsman dear ;
Best of all pools the fowler loves
   The great Volsinian mere.

VII.

But now no stroke of woodman 50
    Is heard by Auser's rill;
No hunter tracks the stag's green path
    Up the Ciminian hill;
Unwatched along Clitumnus
    Grazes the milk-white steer; 55
Unharmed the water-fowl may dip
    In the Volsinian mere.

VIII.

The harvests of Arretium
    This year old men shall reap;
This year young boys in Umbro 60
    Shall plunge the struggling sheep;
And in the vats of Luna
    This year the must shall foam
Round the white feet of laughing girls,
    Whose sires have marched to Rome. 65

IX.

There be thirty chosen prophets,
    The wisest of the land,
Who alway by Lars Porsena
    Both morn and evening stand;
Evening and morn the Thirty 70
    Have turned the verses o'er,
Traced from the right on linen white
    By mighty seers of yore.

X.

And with one voice the Thirty
    Have their glad answer given: 75

"Go forth, go forth, Lars Porsena;
  Go forth, beloved of Heaven;
Go, and return in glory
  To Clusium's royal dome,
And hang round Nurscia's altars   80
  The golden shields of Rome."

XI.

And now hath every city
  Sent up her tale of men;
The foot are fourscore thousand,
  The horse are thousands ten.   85
Before the gates of Sutrium
  Is met the great array.
A proud man was Lars Porsena
  Upon the trysting day.

XII.

For all the Etruscan armies   90
  Were ranged beneath his eye,
And many a banished Roman,
  And many a stout ally;
And with a mighty following
  To join the muster came   95
The Tusculan Mamilius,
  Prince of the Latian name.

XIII.

But by the yellow Tiber
  Was tumult and affright;
From all the spacious champaign   100
  To Rome men took their flight.

A mile around the city
  The throng stopped up the ways;
A fearful sight it was to see
  Through two long nights and days. 105

XIV.

For aged folk on crutches,
  And women great with child,
And mothers sobbing over babes
  That clung to them and smiled,
And sick men borne in litters 110
  High on the necks of slaves,
And troops of sunburnt husbandmen
  With reaping-hooks and staves,

XV.

And droves of mules and asses
  Laden with skins of wine, 115
And endless flocks of goats and sheep,
  And endless herds of kine,
And endless trains of wagons,
  That creaked beneath the weight
Of corn-sacks and of household goods, 120
  Choked every roaring gate.

XVI.

Now from the rock Tarpeian
  Could the wan burghers spy
The line of blazing villages
  Red in the midnight sky. 125
The Fathers of the City
  They sat all night and day,
For every hour some horseman came
  With tidings of dismay.

XVII.

To eastward and to westward
    Have spread the Tuscan bands ;
Nor house nor fence nor dovecote
    In Crustumerium stands.
Verbenna down to Ostia
    Hath wasted all the plain ;
Astur hath stormed Janiculum,
    And the stout guards are slain.

XVIII.

I wis, in all the Senate
    There was no heart so bold
But sore it ached and fast it beat,
    When that ill news was told.
Forthwith uprose the Consul,
    Uprose the Fathers all ;
In haste they girded up their gowns,
    And hied them to the wall.

XIX.

They held a council standing
    Before the River-Gate ;
Short time was there, ye well may guess,
    For musing or debate.
Out spake the Consul roundly :
    "The bridge must straight go down ;
For, since Janiculum is lost,
    Naught else can save the town."

XX.

Just then a scout came flying,
    All wild with haste and fear :

"To arms! to arms! Sir Consul;
 Lars Porsena is here."
On the low hills to westward
 The Consul fixed his eye,
And saw the swarthy storm of dust 160
 Rise fast along the sky.

XXI.

And nearer fast and nearer
 Doth the red whirlwind come;
And louder still and still more loud,
From underneath that rolling cloud, 165
Is heard the trumpet's war-note proud,
 The trampling and the hum.
And plainly and more plainly
 Now through the gloom appears,
Far to left and far to right, 170
In broken gleams of dark-blue light,
The long array of helmets bright,
 The long array of spears.

XXII.

And plainly and more plainly,
 Above that glimmering line, 175
Now might ye see the banners
 Of twelve fair cities shine;
But the banner of proud Clusium
 Was highest of them all,
The terror of the Umbrian, 180
 The terror of the Gaul.

XXIII.

And plainly and more plainly
 Now might the burghers know,

By port and vest, by horse and crest,
    Each warlike Lucumo.
There Cilnius of Arretium
    On his fleet roan was seen;
And Astur of the fourfold shield,
Girt with the brand none else may wield,
Tolumnius with the belt of gold,
And dark Verbenna from the hold
    By reedy Thrasymene.

XXIV.

Fast by the royal standard,
    O'erlooking all the war,
Lars Porsena of Clusium
    Sat in his ivory car.
By the right wheel rode Mamilius,
    Prince of the Latian name;
And by the left false Sextus,
    That wrought the deed of shame.

XXV.

But when the face of Sextus
    Was seen among the foes,
A yell that rent the firmament
    From all the town arose.
On the house-tops was no woman
    But spat towards him and hissed,
No child but screamed out curses
    And shook its little fist.

XXVI.

But the Consul's brow was sad,
    And the Consul's speech was low,

And darkly looked he at the wall,
  And darkly at the foe.
"Their van will be upon us
  Before the bridge goes down;
And if they once may win the bridge, 215
  What hope to save the town?"

XXVII.

Then out spake brave Horatius,
  The Captain of the Gate:
"To every man upon this earth
  Death cometh soon or late. 220
And how can man die better
  Than facing fearful odds,
For the ashes of his fathers
  And the temples of his Gods,

XXVIII.

"And for the tender mother 225
  Who dandled him to rest,
And for the wife who nurses
  His baby at her breast,
And for the holy maidens
  Who feed the eternal flame, 230
To save them from false Sextus
  That wrought the deed of shame?

XXIX.

"Hew down the bridge, Sir Consul,
  With all the speed ye may;
I, with two more to help me, 235
  Will hold the foe in play.

In yon strait path a thousand
  May well be stopped by three.
Now who will stand on either hand,
  And keep the bridge with me?"   240

XXX.

Then out spake Spurius Lartius —
  A Ramnian proud was he:
"Lo, I will stand at thy right hand,
  And keep the bridge with thee."
And out spake strong Herminius —   245
  Of Titian blood was he:
"I will abide on thy left side,
  And keep the bridge with thee."

XXXI.

"Horatius," quoth the Consul,
  "As thou sayest, so let it be."   250
And straight against that great array
  Forth went the dauntless Three.
For Romans in Rome's quarrel
  Spared neither land nor gold,
Nor son nor wife, nor limb nor life,   255
  In the brave days of old.

XXXII.

Then none was for a party;
  Then all were for the State;
Then the great man helped the poor,
  And the poor man loved the great;   260
Then lands were fairly portioned;
  Then spoils were fairly sold:
The Romans were like brothers
  In the brave days of old.

XXXIII.

Now Roman is to Roman 265
   More hateful than a foe;
And the Tribunes beard the high,
   And the Fathers grind the low.
As we wax hot in faction,
   In battle we wax cold; 270
Wherefore men fight not as they fought
   In the brave days of old.

XXXIV.

Now while the Three were tightening
   Their harness on their backs,
The Consul was the foremost man 275
   To take in hand an axe;
And Fathers mixed with Commons
   Seized hatchet, bar, and crow,
And smote upon the planks above,
   And loosed the props below. 280

XXXV.

Meanwhile the Tuscan army,
   Right glorious to behold,
Came flashing back the noonday light,
Rank behind rank, like surges bright
   Of a broad sea of gold. 285
Four hundred trumpets sounded
   A peal of warlike glee,
As that great host, with measured tread,
And spears advanced and ensigns spread,
Rolled slowly towards the bridge's head, 290
   Where stood the dauntless Three.

XXXVI.

The Three stood calm and silent,
   And looked upon the foes,
And a great shout of laughter
   From all the vanguard rose;   295
And forth three chiefs came spurring
   Before that deep array;
To earth they sprang, their swords they drew,
And lifted high their shields, and flew
   To win the narrow way;   300

XXXVII.

Aunus from green Tifernum,
   Lord of the Hill of Vines;
And Seius, whose eight hundred slaves
   Sicken in Ilva's mines;
And Picus, long to Clusium   305
   Vassal in peace and war,
Who led to fight his Umbrian powers
From that grey crag where, girt with towers,
The fortress of Nequinum lowers
   O'er the pale waves of Nar.   310

XXXVIII.

Stout Lartius hurled down Aunus
   Into the stream beneath;
Herminius struck at Seius,
   And clove him to the teeth;
At Picus brave Horatius   315
   Darted one fiery thrust,
And the proud Umbrian's gilded arms
   Clashed in the bloody dust.

XXXIX.

Then Ocnus of Falerii
  Rushed on the Roman Three;
And Lausulus of Urgo,
  The rover of the sea;
And Aruns of Volsinium,
  Who slew the great wild boar,
The great wild boar that had his den
Amidst the reeds of Cosa's fen,
And wasted fields and slaughtered men
  Along Albinia's shore.

XL.

Herminius smote down Aruns;
  Lartius laid Ocnus low;
Right to the heart of Lausulus
  Horatius sent a blow.
"Lie there," he cried, "fell pirate!
  No more, aghast and pale,
From Ostia's walls the crowd shall mark
The track of thy destroying bark.
No more Campania's hinds shall fly
To woods and caverns, when they spy
  Thy thrice accursed sail."

XLI.

But now no sound of laughter
  Was heard among the foes;
A wild and wrathful clamor
  From all the vanguard rose.
Six spears' length from the entrance
  Halted that deep array,

And for a space no man came forth
  To win the narrow way.

XLII.

But hark! the cry is "Astur!"
  And lo! the ranks divide,
And the great Lord of Luna   350
  Comes with his stately stride.
Upon his ample shoulders
  Clangs loud the fourfold shield,
And in his hand he shakes the brand
  Which none but he can wield.   355

XLIII.

He smiled on those bold Romans
  A smile serene and high;
He eyed the flinching Tuscans,
  And scorn was in his eye.
Quoth he, "The she-wolf's litter   360
  Stand savagely at bay;
But will ye dare to follow,
  If Astur clears the way?"

XLIV.

Then, whirling up his broadsword
  With both hands to the height,   365
He rushed against Horatius,
  And smote with all his might.
With shield and blade Horatius
  Right deftly turned the blow.
The blow, though turned, came yet too nigh;   370
It missed his helm, but gashed his thigh;
The Tuscans raised a joyful cry
  To see the red blood flow.

XLV.

He reeled, and on Herminius
    He leaned one breathing-space;   375
Then, like a wildcat mad with wounds,
    Sprang right at Astur's face;
Through teeth and skull and helmet
    So fierce a thrust he sped,
The good sword stood a hand-breadth out   380
    Behind the Tuscan's head.

XLVI.

And the great Lord of Luna
    Fell at that deadly stroke,
As falls on Mount Alvernus
    A thunder-smitten oak.   385
Far o'er the crashing forest
    The giant arms lie spread;
And the pale augurs, muttering low,
    Gaze on the blasted head.

XLVII.

On Astur's throat Horatius   390
    Right firmly pressed his heel,
And thrice and four times tugged amain,
    Ere he wrenched out the steel.
"And see," he cried, "the welcome,
    Fair guests, that waits you here!   395
What noble Lucumo comes next
    To taste our Roman cheer?"

XLVIII.

But at his haughty challenge
    A sullen murmur ran,

Mingled of wrath and shame and dread, 400
    Along that glittering van.
There lacked not men of prowess
    Nor men of lordly race;
For all Etruria's noblest
    Were round the fatal place. 405

XLIX.

But all Etruria's noblest
    Felt their hearts sink to see
On the earth the bloody corpses,
    In the path the dauntless Three;
And from the ghastly entrance 410
    Where those bold Romans stood
All shrank, like boys who, unaware,
Ranging the woods to start a hare,
Come to the mouth of the dark lair
Where, growling low, a fierce old bear 415
    Lies amidst bones and blood.

L.

Was none who would be foremost
    To lead such dire attack;
But those behind cried "Forward!"
    And those before cried "Back!" 420
And backward now and forward
    Wavers the deep array;
And on the tossing sea of steel
    To and fro the standards reel,
And the victorious trumpet-peal 425
    Dies fitfully away.

LI.

Yet one man for one moment
    Stood out before the crowd;

Well known was he to all the Three,
    And they gave him greeting loud:
"Now welcome, welcome, Sextus!
    Now welcome to thy home!
Why dost thou stay and turn away?
    Here lies the road to Rome."

LII.

Thrice looked he at the city,
    Thrice looked he at the dead;
And thrice came on in fury,
    And thrice turned back in dread:
And, white with fear and hatred,
    Scowled at the narrow way,
Where, wallowing in a pool of blood,
    The bravest Tuscans lay.

LIII.

But meanwhile axe and lever
    Have manfully been plied,
And now the bridge hangs tottering
    Above the boiling tide.
"Come back, come back, Horatius!"
    Loud cried the Fathers all.
"Back, Lartius! back, Herminius!
    Back, ere the ruin fall!"

LIV.

Back darted Spurius Lartius,
    Herminius darted back;
And, as they passed, beneath their feet
    They felt the timbers crack.
But when they turned their faces,
    And on the farther shore

Saw brave Horatius stand alone,
    They would have crossed once more.

LV.

But with a crash like thunder
    Fell every loosened beam,   460
And, like a dam, the mighty wreck
    Lay right athwart the stream.
And a long shout of triumph
    Rose from the walls of Rome,
As to the highest turret-tops   465
    Was splashed the yellow foam.

LVI.

And, like a horse unbroken
    When first he feels the rein,
The furious river struggled hard,
    And tossed his tawny mane,   470
And burst the curb and bounded,
    Rejoicing to be free,
And, whirling down in fierce career
Battlement and plank and pier,
    Rushed headlong to the sea.   475

LVII.

Alone stood brave Horatius,
    But constant still in mind,
Thrice thirty thousand foes before
    And the broad flood behind.
"Down with him!" cried false Sextus,   480
    With a smile on his pale face.
"Now yield thee," cried Lars Porsena,
    "Now yield thee to our grace."

LVIII.

Round turned he, as not deigning
   Those craven ranks to see;   485
Naught spake he to Lars Porsena,
   To Sextus naught spake he;
But he saw on Palatinus
   The white porch of his home,
And he spake to the noble river   490
   That rolls by the towers of Rome:

LIX.

"O Tiber! father Tiber!
   To whom the Romans pray,
A Roman's life, a Roman's arms,
   Take thou in charge this day!"   495
So he spake, and speaking sheathed
   The good sword by his side,
And with his harness on his back
   Plunged headlong in the tide.

LX.

No sound of joy or sorrow   500
   Was heard from either bank,
But friends and foes in dumb surprise,
With parted lips and straining eyes,
   Stood gazing where he sank;
And when above the surges   505
   They saw his crest appear,
All Rome sent forth a rapturous cry,
And even the ranks of Tuscany
   Could scarce forbear to cheer.

LXI.

But fiercely ran the current,
    Swollen high by months of rain;
And fast his blood was flowing,
    And he was sore in pain,
And heavy with his armor,
    And spent with changing blows;
And oft they thought him sinking,
    But still again he rose.

LXII.

Never, I ween, did swimmer,
    In such an evil case,
Struggle through such a raging flood
    Safe to the landing place;
But his limbs were borne up bravely
    By the brave heart within,
And our good father Tiber
    Bare bravely up his chin.

LXIII.

"Curse on him!" quoth false Sextus;
    "Will not the villain drown?
But for this stay, ere close of day
    We should have sacked the town!"
"Heaven help him!" quoth Lars Porsena,
    "And bring him safe to shore;
For such a gallant feat of arms
    Was never seen before."

LXIV.

And now he feels the bottom;
    Now on dry earth he stands;

Now round him throng the Fathers
  To press his gory hands;
And now, with shouts and clapping
  And noise of weeping loud,
He enters through the River-Gate,   540
  Borne by the joyous crowd.

LXV.

They gave him of the corn-land,
  That was of public right,
As much as two strong oxen
  Could plough from morn till night;   545
And they made a molten image
  And set it up on high,
And there it stands unto this day
  To witness if I lie.

LXVI.

It stands in the Comitium,   550
  Plain for all folk to see,
Horatius in his harness
  Halting upon one knee;
And underneath is written
  In letters all of gold   555
How valiantly he kept the bridge
  In the brave days of old.

LXVII.

And still his name sounds stirring
  Unto the men of Rome,
As the trumpet-blast that cries to them   560
  To charge the Volscian home;
And wives still pray to Juno

For boys with hearts as bold
As his who kept the bridge so well
  In the brave days of old.

LXVIII.

And in the nights of winter,
  When the cold north winds blow,
And the long howling of the wolves
  Is heard amidst the snow;
When round the lonely cottage
  Roars loud the tempest's din,
And the good logs of Algidus
  Roar louder yet within;

LXIX.

When the oldest cask is opened,
  And the largest lamp is lit;
When the chestnuts glow in the embers,
  And the kid turns on the spit;
When young and old in circle
  Around the firebrands close;
When the girls are weaving baskets,
  And the lads are shaping bows;

LXX.

When the goodman mends his armor,
  And trims his helmet's plume;
When the goodwife's shuttle merrily
  Goes flashing through the loom;
With weeping and with laughter
  Still is the story told,
How well Horatius kept the bridge
  In the brave days of old.

THE
BATTLE OF THE LAKE REGILLUS.

THE following poem is supposed to have been produced about ninety years after the lay of Horatius. Some persons mentioned in the lay of Horatius make their appearance again, and some appellations and epithets used in the lay of Horatius have been purposely repeated; for, in an age of ballad poetry, it scarcely ever fails to happen that certain phrases come to be appropriated to certain men and things, and are regularly applied to those men and things by every minstrel. Thus we find, both in the Homeric poems and in Hesiod, βίη Ἡρακληείη, περικλυτὸς Ἀμφιγυήεις, διάκτορος Ἀργειφόντης, ἑπτάπυλος Θήβη, Ἑλένης ἕνεκ᾽ ἠυκόμοιο. Thus, too, in our own national songs Douglas is almost always the doughty Douglas, England is merry England, all the gold is red, and all the ladies are gay.

The principal distinction between the lay of Horatius and the lay of the Lake Regillus is that the former is meant to be purely Roman, while the latter, though national in its general spirit, has a slight tincture of Greek learning and of Greek superstition. The story of the Tarquins, as it has come down to us, appears to have been compiled from the works of several popular poets; and one, at least, of those poets appears to have visited the Greek colonies in Italy, if not Greece itself, and to have had some acquaintance with the works of Homer and Herodotus. Many of the most striking adventures of the house of Tarquin, before Lucretia makes her appearance, have a Greek character. The Tarquins themselves are represented as Corinthian nobles of the great house of the Bacchiadæ, driven from their country by the tyranny of that Cypselus the tale of whose strange escape Herodotus has related with incomparable simplicity and liveliness.[1] Livy and Dionysius tell us that, when Tarquin the Proud was asked what was the best mode of governing a conquered city, he replied only by beating down with his staff all the tallest poppies in his garden.[2] This is exactly what Herodotus, in the passage to which reference has already been made, relates of the counsel given to Periander, the son of Cypselus. The stratagem by which the town of Gabii is brought under the power of the Tarquins is, again, obviously copied from Herodotus.[3] The embassy of the young Tarquins to the oracle at Delphi is just such a story as would be told by a poet whose head was full of the Greek mythology; and the ambiguous answer returned by Apollo is in the exact style of the prophecies which, according to Herodotus, lured Crœsus to destruction. Then the character of the narrative changes. From the first mention of Lucretia to the retreat of Porsena nothing seems to be borrowed from foreign sources. The villainy of Sextus, the suicide of his victim, the revolution, the death of the sons of Brutus, the defence of the bridge, Mucius burning his hand,[4] Clœlia swimming through Tiber, seem to be all strictly Roman. But when we have done with the Tuscan war, and enter upon the war with the Latines, we are again struck by the Greek air of the story. The Battle of the

---

[1] Herodotus, v. 92.   Livy, i. 34.   Dionysius, iii. 46.

[2] Livy, i. 54.   Dionysius, iv. 56.

[3] Herodotus, iii. 154.   Livy, i. 53.

[4] M. de Pouilly attempted, a hundred and twenty years ago, to prove that the story of Mucius was of Greek origin; but he was signally confuted by the Abbé Sallier. See the *Mémoires de l'Académie des Inscriptions*, vi. 27. 66.

Lake Regillus is in all respects a Homeric battle, except that the combatants ride astride on their horses instead of driving chariots. The mass of fighting men is hardly mentioned. The leaders single each other out, and engage hand to hand. The great object of the warriors on both sides is, as in the Iliad, to obtain possession of the spoils and bodies of the slain; and several circumstances are related which forcibly remind us of the great slaughter round the corpses of Sarpedon and Patroclus.

But there is one circumstance which deserves especial notice. Both the war of Troy and the war of Regillus were caused by the licentious passions of young princes, who were therefore peculiarly bound not to be sparing of their own persons in the day of battle. Now the conduct of Sextus at Regillus, as described by Livy, so exactly resembles that of Paris, as described at the beginning of the third book of the Iliad, that it is difficult to believe the resemblance accidental. Paris appears before the Trojan ranks, defying the bravest Greek to encounter him:

Τρωσὶν μὲν προμάχιζεν Ἀλέξανδρος θεοειδής,
 . . . Ἀργείων προκαλίζετο πάντας ἀρίστους,
ἀντίβιον μαχέσασθαι ἐν αἰνῇ δηϊοτῆτι.

Livy introduces Sextus in a similar manner: "Ferocem juvenem Tarquinium, ostentantem se in prima exsulum acie." Menelaus rushes to meet Paris. A Roman noble, eager for vengeance, spurs his horse towards Sextus. Both the guilty princes are instantly terror stricken:

Τὸν δ' ὡς οὖν ἐνόησεν Ἀλέξανδρος θεοειδὴς
ἐν προμάχοισι φανέντα, κατεπλήγη φίλον ἦτορ·
ἂψ δ' ἑτάρων εἰς ἔθνος ἐχάζετο κῆρ' ἀλεείνων.

"Tarquinius," says Livy, "retro in agmen suorum infenso cessit hosti." If this be a fortuitous coincidence, it is one of the most extraordinary in literature.

In the following poem, therefore, images and incidents have been borrowed, not merely without scruple, but on principle, from the incomparable battle-pieces of Homer.

The popular belief at Rome, from an early period, seems to have been that the event of the great day of Regillus was decided by supernatural agency. Castor and Pollux, it was said, had fought, armed and mounted, at the head of the legions of the commonwealth, and had afterwards carried the news of the victory with incredible speed to the city. The well in the Forum at which they had alighted was pointed out. Near the well rose their ancient temple. A great festival was kept to their honor on the Ides of Quintilis, supposed to be the anniversary of the battle; and on that day sumptuous sacrifices were offered to them at the public charge. One spot on the margin of Lake Regillus was regarded during many ages with superstitious awe. A mark, resembling in shape a horse's hoof, was discernible in the volcanic rock; and this mark was believed to have been made by one of the celestial chargers.

How the legend originated cannot now be ascertained, but we may easily imagine several ways in which it might have originated; nor is it at all necessary to suppose, with Julius Frontinus, that two young men were dressed up by the Dictator to personate the sons of Leda. It is probable that Livy is correct when he says that the Roman general, in the hour of peril, vowed a temple to Castor. If so, nothing could be more natural than that the multitude should ascribe the victory to the favor of the Twin Gods. When such was the prevailing sentiment, any man who chose to declare that, in the midst of the confusion and slaughter, he had seen two godlike forms on white horses scattering the Latines would find ready credence. We know, indeed, that in modern times a very similar story actually found credence among a people much more civilized than the Romans of the fifth century before Christ. A chaplain of Cortes, writing about thirty years after the conquest of Mexico, in an age of printing presses, libraries, universities, scholars, logicians, jurists, and statesmen, had the face to assert that, in one engagement against the Indians, Saint James had appeared on a gray horse at the head of the Castilian adventurers. Many of those adventurers were living when this lie was printed. One of them, honest Bernal Diaz, wrote an account of the expedition. He had the evidence of his own senses against the legend; but he seems to have distrusted even the evidence of his own senses. He says that he was in the battle, and that he saw a gray horse with a man on his back, but that the man was, to his thinking, Francesco de Morla, and not the ever-blessed apostle Saint James. "Nevertheless," Bernal adds, "it may be that the person on the gray horse was the glorious apostle Saint James, and that I, sinner that I am, was unworthy to see him." The Romans of the age of Cincinnatus were probably quite as credulous as the Spanish subjects of Charles the Fifth. It is therefore conceivable that the appearance of Castor and Pollux may have become an article of faith before the generation which had fought at Regillus had passed away. Nor could anything be more natural than that the poets of the next age should embellish this story, and make the celestial horsemen bear the tidings of victory to Rome.

Many years after the temple of the Twin Gods had been built in the Forum, an important addition was made to the ceremonial by which the state annually testified its gratitude for their protection. Quintus Fabius and Publius Decius were elected Censors at a momentous crisis.

It had become absolutely necessary that the classification of the citizens should be revised. On that classification depended the distribution of political power. Party-spirit ran high; and the republic seemed to be in danger of falling under the dominion either of a narrow oligarchy or of an ignorant and headstrong rabble. Under such circumstances, the most illustrious patrician and the most illustrious plebeian of the age were entrusted with the office of arbitrating between the angry factions; and they performed their arduous task to the satisfaction of all honest and reasonable men.

One of their reforms was a remodelling of the equestrian order; and, having effected this reform, they determined to give to their work a sanction derived from religion. In the chivalrous societies of modern times, societies which have much more than may at first sight appear in common with the equestrian order of Rome, it has been usual to invoke the special protection of some Saint, and to observe his day with peculiar solemnity. Thus the Companions of the Garter wear the image of Saint George depending from their collars, and meet on great occasions in Saint George's Chapel. Thus, when Lewis the Fourteenth instituted a new order of chivalry for the rewarding of military merit, he commended it to the favor of his own glorified ancestor and patron, and decreed that all the members of the fraternity should meet at the royal palace on the feast of Saint Lewis, should attend the king to chapel, should hear mass, and should subsequently hold their great annual assembly. There is a considerable resemblance between this rule of the order of Saint Lewis and the rule which Fabius and Decius made respecting the Roman Knights. It was ordained that a grand muster and inspection of the equestrian body should be part of the ceremonial performed, on the anniversary of the

battle of Regillus, in honor of Castor and Pollux, the
two equestrian Gods. All the Knights, clad in purple
and crowned with olive, were to meet at a temple of Mars
in the suburbs. Thence they were to ride in state to the
Forum, where the temple of the Twins stood. This pageant was, during several centuries, considered as one of
the most splendid sights of Rome. In the time of Dionysius the cavalcade sometimes consisted of five thousand
horsemen, all persons of fair repute and easy fortune.[1]

There can be no doubt that the Censors who instituted
this august ceremony acted in concert with the Pontiffs,
to whom, by the constitution of Rome, the superintend-
ence of the public worship belonged; and it is probable
that those high religious functionaries were, as usual, fortunate enough to find in their books or traditions some
warrant for the innovation.

The following poem is supposed to have been made for
this great occasion. Songs, we know, were chanted at
the religious festivals of Rome from an early period, —
indeed from so early a period that some of the sacred
verses were popularly ascribed to Numa, and were utterly
unintelligible in the age of Augustus. In the Second
Punic War a great feast was held in honor of Juno, and
a song was sung in her praise. This song was extant
when Livy wrote; and, though exceedingly rugged and
uncouth, seemed to him not wholly destitute of merit.[2]
A song, as we learn from Horace,[3] was part of the established ritual at the great Secular Jubilee. It is therefore
likely that the Censors and Pontiffs, when they had

---

[1] See Livy, ix. 46. Val. Max. ii. 2. Aurel. Vict. *De Viris Illustribus*, 32. Dionysius, vi. 13. Plin. *Hist. Nat.* xv. 5. See also the singularly ingenious chapter in Niebuhr's posthumous volume, *Die Censur des Q. Fabius und P. Decius.*

[2] Livy, xxvii. 37.   [3] Hor. *Carmen Saeculare.*

resolved to add a grand procession of Knights to the other solemnities annually performed on the Ides of Quintilis, would call in the aid of a poet. Such a poet would naturally take for his subject the battle of Regillus, the appearance of the Twin Gods, and the institution of their festival. He would find abundant materials in the ballads of his predecessors; and he would make free use of the scanty stock of Greek learning which he had himself acquired. He would probably introduce some wise and holy Pontiff enjoining the magnificent ceremonial, which after a long interval had at length been adopted. If the poem succeeded, many persons would commit it to memory. Parts of it would be sung to the pipe at banquets. It would be peculiarly interesting to the great Posthumian House, which numbered among its many images that of the Dictator Aulus, the hero of Regillus. The orator who, in the following generation, pronounced the funeral panegyric over the remains of Lucius Posthumius Megellus, thrice Consul, would borrow largely from the lay; and thus some passages, much disfigured, would probably find their way into the chronicles which were afterwards in the hands of Dionysius and Livy.

Antiquaries differ widely as to the situation of the field of battle. The opinion of those who suppose that the armies met near Cornufelle, between Frascati and the Monte Porzio, is at least plausible, and has been followed in the poem.

As to the details of the battle, it has not been thought desirable to adhere minutely to the accounts which have come down to us. Those accounts, indeed, differ widely from each other, and in all probability differ as widely from the ancient poem from which they were originally derived.

It is unnecessary to point out the obvious imitations of the Iliad, which have been purposely introduced.

THE BATTLE OF THE LAKE REGILLUS.

A LAY SUNG AT THE FEAST OF CASTOR AND POLLUX, ON THE IDES OF QUINTILIS, IN THE YEAR OF THE CITY CCCCLI.

I.

Ho, trumpets, sound a war-note!
    Ho, lictors, clear the way!
The Knights will ride in all their pride
    Along the streets to-day.
To-day the doors and windows   5
    Are hung with garlands all,
From Castor in the Forum
    To Mars without the wall.
Each Knight is robed in purple,
    With olive each is crowned;   10
A gallant war-horse under each
    Paws haughtily the ground.
While flows the Yellow River,
    While stands the Sacred Hill,
The proud Ides of Quintilis   15
    Shall have such honor still.
Gay are the Martian Kalends,
    December's Nones are gay;
But the proud Ides, when the squadron rides,
    Shall be Rome's whitest day.   20

II.

Unto the Great Twin Brethren
    We keep this solemn feast.
Swift, swift, the Great Twin Brethren
    Came spurring from the east.

They came o'er wild Parthenius 25
   Tossing in waves of pine,
O'er Cirrha's dome, o'er Adria's foam,
   O'er purple Apennine;
From where with flutes and dances
   Their ancient mansion rings 30
In lordly Lacedæmon,
   The city of two kings,
To where, by Lake Regillus,
   Under the Porcian height,
All in the lands of Tusculum, 35
   Was fought the glorious fight.

III.

Now on the place of slaughter
   Are cots and sheepfolds seen,
And rows of vines and fields of wheat
   And apple-orchards green; 40
The swine crush the big acorns
   That fall from Corne's oaks;
Upon the turf by the Fair Fount
   The reaper's pottage smokes.
The fisher baits his angle, 45
   The hunter twangs his bow;
Little they think on those strong limbs
   That moulder deep below.
Little they think how sternly
   That day the trumpets pealed; 50
How in the slippery swamp of blood
   Warrior and war-horse reeled;
How wolves came with fierce gallop,
   And crows on eager wings,
To tear the flesh of captains, 55
   And peck the eyes of kings;

How thick the dead lay scattered
   Under the Porcian height;
How through the gates of Tusculum
   Raved the wild stream of flight;   60
And how the Lake Regillus
   Bubbled with crimson foam,
What time the Thirty Cities
   Came forth to war with Rome.

IV.

But, Roman, when thou standest   65
   Upon that holy ground,
Look thou with heed on the dark rock
   That girds the dark lake round;
So shalt thou see a hoof-mark
   Stamped deep into the flint;   70
It was no hoof of mortal steed
   That made so strange a dint.
There to the Great Twin Brethren
   Vow thou thy vows, and pray
That they, in tempest and in fight,   75
   Will keep thy head alway.

V.

Since last the Great Twin Brethren
   Of mortal eyes were seen,
Have years gone by an hundred
   And fourscore and thirteen.   80
That summer a Virginius
   Was Consul first in place;
The second was stout Aulus,
   Of the Posthumian race.
The Herald of the Latines   85
   From Gabii came in state;

The Herald of the Latines
    Passed through Rome's Eastern Gate;
The Herald of the Latines
    Did in our Forum stand,
And there he did his office,
    A sceptre in his hand:

VI.

" Hear, Senators and people
    Of the good town of Rome,
The Thirty Cities charge you
    To bring the Tarquins home;
And if ye still be stubborn
    To work the Tarquins wrong,
The Thirty Cities warn you,
    Look that your walls be strong."

VII.

Then spake the Consul Aulus —
    He spake a bitter jest —
" Once the jays sent a message
    Unto the eagle's nest:
' Now yield thou up thine eyrie
    Unto the carrion-kite,
Or come forth valiantly and face
    The jays in deadly fight.'
Forth looked in wrath the eagle;
    And carrion-kite and jay,
Soon as they saw his beak and claw,
    Fled screaming far away."

VIII.

The Herald of the Latines
    Hath hied him back in state;

The Fathers of the City
    Are met in high debate.
Then spake the elder Consul,
    An ancient man and wise:
"Now hearken, Conscript Fathers,
    To that which I advise.
In seasons of great peril
    'Tis good that one bear sway;
Then choose we a Dictator,
    Whom all men shall obey.
Camerium knows how deeply
    The sword of Aulus bites,
And all our city calls him
    The man of seventy fights.
Then let him be Dictator
    For six months and no more,
And have a Master of the Knights,
    And axes twenty-four."

IX.

So Aulus was Dictator,
    The man of seventy fights;
He made Æbutius Elva
    His Master of the Knights.
On the third morn thereafter,
    At dawning of the day,
Did Aulus and Æbutius
    Set forth with their array.
Sempronius Atratinus
    Was left in charge at home
With boys and with gray-headed men
    To keep the walls of Rome.
Hard by the Lake Regillus
    Our camp was pitched at night;

Eastward a mile the Latines lay,
　Under the Porcian height.
Far over hill and valley
　Their mighty host was spread,　　　　150
And with their thousand watch-fires
　The midnight sky was red.

X.

Up rose the golden morning
　Over the Porcian height,
The proud Ides of Quintilis　　　　155
　Marked evermore with white.
Not without secret trouble
　Our bravest saw the foes;
For girt by threescore thousand spears
　The thirty standards rose.　　　　160
From every warlike city
　That boasts the Latian name,
Foredoomed to dogs and vultures,
　That gallant army came:
From Setia's purple vineyards,　　　　165
　From Norba's ancient wall,
From the white streets of Tusculum,
　The proudest town of all;
From where the Witch's Fortress
　O'erhangs the dark-blue seas;　　　　170
From the still glassy lake that sleeps
　Beneath Aricia's trees —
Those trees in whose dim shadow
　The ghastly priest doth reign,
The priest who slew the slayer,　　　　175
　And shall himself be slain;
From the drear banks of Ufens,
　Where flights of marsh-fowl play,

And buffaloes lie wallowing
  Through the hot summer's day;
From the gigantic watch-towers,
  No work of earthly men,
Whence Cora's sentinels o'erlook
  The never-ending fen;
From the Laurentian jungle,
  The wild hog's reedy home;
From the green steeps whence Anio leaps
  In floods of snow-white foam.

XI.

Aricia, Cora, Norba,
  Velitræ, with the might
Of Setia and of Tusculum,
  Were marshalled on the right.
Their leader was Mamilius,
  Prince of the Latian name;
Upon his head a helmet
  Of red gold shone like flame;
High on a gallant charger
  Of dark-gray hue he rode;
Over his gilded armor
  A vest of purple flowed,
Woven in the land of sunrise
  By Syria's dark-browed daughters,
And by the sails of Carthage brought
  Far o'er the southern waters.

XII.

Lavinium and Laurentum
  Had on the left their post,
With all the banners of the marsh
  And banners of the coast.

Their leader was false Sextus,
    That wrought the deed of shame;   210
With restless pace and haggard face
    To his last field he came.
Men said he saw strange visions
    Which none beside might see,
And that strange sounds were in his ears   215
    Which none might hear but he.
A woman fair and stately,
    But pale as are the dead,
Oft through the watches of the night
    Sat spinning by his bed.   220
And as she plied the distaff,
    In a sweet voice and low
She sang of great old houses
    And fights fought long ago.
So spun she and so sang she   225
    Until the east was gray,
Then pointed to her bleeding breast,
    And shrieked, and fled away.

XIII.

But in the centre thickest
    Were ranged the shields of foes,   230
And from the centre loudest
    The cry of battle rose.
There Tibur marched and Pedum
    Beneath proud Tarquin's rule,
And Ferentinum of the rock,   235
    And Gabii of the pool.
There rode the Volscian succors;
    There, in a dark stern ring,
The Roman exiles gathered close
    Around the ancient king.   240

Though white as Mount Soracte,
    When winter nights are long,
His beard flowed down o'er mail and belt,
    His heart and hand were strong;
Under his hoary eyebrows 245
    Still flashed forth quenchless rage,
And, if the lance shook in his gripe,
    'T was more with hate than age.
Close at his side was Titus
    On an Apulian steed— 250
Titus, the youngest Tarquin,
    Too good for such a breed.

XIV.

Now on each side the leaders
    Give signal for the charge;
And on each side the footmen 255
    Strode on with lance and targe;
And on each side the horsemen
    Struck their spurs deep in gore,
And front to front the armies
    Met with a mighty roar; 260
And under that great battle
    The earth with blood was red;
And, like the Pomptine fog at morn,
    The dust hung overhead;
And louder still and louder 265
    Rose from the darkened field
The braying of the war-horns,
    The clang of sword and shield,
The rush of squadrons sweeping
    Like whirlwinds o'er the plain, 270
The shouting of the slayers
    And screeching of the slain.

XV.

False Sextus rode out foremost,
    His look was high and bold;
His corslet was of bison's hide,   275
    Plated with steel and gold.
As glares the famished eagle
    From the Digentian rock
On a choice lamb that bounds alone
    Before Bandusia's flock,   280
Herminius glared on Sextus
    And came with eagle speed,
Herminius on black Auster,
    Brave champion on brave steed;
In his right hand the broadsword   285
    That kept the bridge so well,
And on his helm the crown he won
    When proud Fidenæ fell.
Woe to the maid whose lover
    Shall cross his path to-day!   290
False Sextus saw and trembled,
    And turned and fled away.
As turns, as flies, the woodman
    In the Calabrian brake,
When through the reeds gleams the round eye 295
    Of that fell speckled snake,
So turned, so fled, false Sextus,
    And hid him in the rear,
Behind the dark Lavinian ranks
    Bristling with crest and spear.   300

XVI.

But far to north Æbutius,
    The Master of the Knights,

Gave Tubero of Norba
    To feed the Porcian kites.
Next under those red horse-hoofs   305
    Flaccus of Setia lay;
Better had he been pruning
    Among his elms that day.
Mamilius saw the slaughter,
    And tossed his golden crest,   310
And towards the Master of the Knights
    Through the thick battle pressed.
Æbutius smote Mamilius
    So fiercely on the shield
That the great lord of Tusculum   315
    Well nigh rolled on the field.
Mamilius smote Æbutius,
    With a good aim and true,
Just where the neck and shoulder join,
    And pierced him through and through;   320
And brave Æbutius Elva
    Fell swooning to the ground,
But a thick wall of bucklers
    Encompassed him around.
His clients from the battle   325
    Bare him some little space,
And filled a helm from the dark lake,
    And bathed his brow and face;
And when at last he opened
    His swimming eyes to light,   330
Men say the earliest word he spake
    Was, "Friends, how goes the fight?"

XVII.

But meanwhile in the centre
    Great deeds of arms were wrought;

There Aulus the Dictator 335
 And there Valerius fought.
Aulus with his good broadsword
 A bloody passage cleared
To where, amidst the thickest foes,
 He saw the long white beard. 340
Flat lighted that good broadsword
 Upon proud Tarquin's head.
He dropped the lance, he dropped the reins;
 He fell as fall the dead.
Down Aulus springs to slay him, 345
 With eyes like coals of fire;
But faster Titus hath sprung down,
 And hath bestrode his sire.
Latian captains, Roman knights,
 Fast down to earth they spring, 350
And hand to hand they fight on foot
 Around the ancient king.
First Titus gave tall Cæso
 A death wound in the face;
Tall Cæso was the bravest man 355
 Of the brave Fabian race;
Aulus slew Rex of Gabii,
 The priest of Juno's shrine:
Valerius smote down Julius,
 Of Rome's great Julian line— 360
Julius, who left his mansion
 High on the Velian hill,
And through all turns of weal and woe
 Followed proud Tarquin still.
Now right across proud Tarquin 365
 A corpse was Julius laid;
And Titus groaned with rage and grief,
 And at Valerius made.

Valerius struck at Titus
  And lopped off half his crest; 370
But Titus stabbed Valerius
  A span deep in the breast.
Like a mast snapped by the tempest,
  Valerius reeled and fell.
Ah! woe is me for the good house 375
  That loves the people well!
Then shouted loud the Latines,
  And with one rush they bore
The struggling Romans backward
  Three lances' length and more; 380
And up they took proud Tarquin
  And laid him on a shield,
And four strong yeomen bare him,
  Still senseless, from the field.

XVIII.

But fiercer grew the fighting 385
  Around Valerius dead;
For Titus dragged him by the foot,
  And Aulus by the head.
"On, Latines, on!" quoth Titus,
  "See how the rebels fly!" 390
"Romans, stand firm!" quoth Aulus,
  "And win this fight or die!
They must not give Valerius
  To raven and to kite;
For aye Valerius loathed the wrong, 395
  And aye upheld the right;
And for your wives and babies
  In the front rank he fell.
Now play the men for the good house
  That loves the people well!" 400

XIX.

Then tenfold round the body
   The roar of battle rose,
Like the roar of a burning forest
   When a strong north wind blows.
Now backward and now forward
   Rocked furiously the fray,
Till none could see Valerius,
   And none wist where he lay.
For shivered arms and ensigns
   Were heaped there in a mound,
And corpses stiff, and dying men
   That writhed and gnawed the ground;
And wounded horses kicking
   And snorting purple foam;
Right well did such a couch befit
   A Consular of Rome.

XX.

But north looked the Dictator;
   North looked he long and hard,
And spake to Caius Cossus,
   The Captain of his Guard:
"Caius, of all the Romans
   Thou hast the keenest sight;
Say, what through yonder storm of dust
   Comes from the Latian right?"

XXI.

Then answered Caius Cossus:
   "I see an evil sight;
The banner of proud Tusculum
   Comes from the Latian right.

I see the plumed horsemen;
    And far before the rest 430
I see the dark-gray charger,
    I see the purple vest,
I see the golden helmet
    That shines far off like flame;
So ever rides Mamilius, 435
    Prince of the Latian name."

XXII.

"Now hearken, Caius Cossus;
    Spring on thy horse's back;
Ride as the wolves of Apennine
    Were all upon thy track; 440
Haste to our southward battle,
    And never draw thy rein
Until thou find Herminius,
    And bid him come amain."

XXIII.

So Aulus spake, and turned him 445
    Again to that fierce strife;
And Caius Cossus mounted,
    And rode for death and life.
Loud clanged beneath his horse-hoofs
    The helmets of the dead, 450
And many a curdling pool of blood
    Splashed him from heel to head.
So came he far to southward,
    Where fought the Roman host
Against the banners of the marsh 455
    And banners of the coast.
Like corn before the sickle
    The stout Lavinians fell

Beneath the edge of the true sword
    That kept the bridge so well.   460

XXIV.

"Herminius, Aulus greets thee;
    He bids thee come with speed
To help our central battle,
    For sore is there our need.
There wars the youngest Tarquin,   465
    And there the Crest of Flame,
The Tusculan Mamilius,
    Prince of the Latian name.
Valerius hath fallen fighting
    In front of our array,   470
And Aulus of the seventy fields
    Alone upholds the day."

XXV.

Herminius beat his bosom,
    But never a word he spake.
He clapped his hand on Auster's mane,   475
    He gave the reins a shake;
Away, away, went Auster
    Like an arrow from the bow:
Black Auster was the fleetest steed
    From Aufidus to Po.   480

XXVI.

Right glad were all the Romans
    Who, in that hour of dread,
Against great odds bare up the war
    Around Valerius dead,
When from the south the cheering   485
    Rose with a mighty swell:

"Herminius comes, Herminius,
   Who kept the bridge so well!"

XXVII.

Mamilius spied Herminius,
   And dashed across the way: 490
"Herminius, I have sought thee
   Through many a bloody day.
One of us two, Herminius,
   Shall never more go home.
I will lay on for Tusculum, 495
   And lay thou on for Rome!"

XXVIII.

All round them paused the battle,
   While met in mortal fray
The Roman and the Tusculan,
   The horses black and gray. 500
Herminius smote Mamilius
   Through breastplate and through breast,
And fast flowed out the purple blood
   Over the purple vest.
Mamilius smote Herminius 505
   Through head-piece and through head:
And side by side those chiefs of pride
   Together fell down dead.
Down fell they dead together
   In a great lake of gore; 510
And still stood all who saw them fall
   While men might count a score.

XXIX.

Fast, fast, with heels wild spurning,
   The dark-gray charger fled:

He burst through ranks of fighting men, 515
  He sprang o'er heaps of dead.
His bridle far outstreaming,
  His flanks all blood and foam,
He sought the southern mountains,
  The mountains of his home. 520
The pass was steep and rugged,
  The wolves they howled and whined;
But he ran like a whirlwind up the pass,
  And he left the wolves behind.
Through many a startled hamlet 525
  Thundered his flying feet;
He rushed through the gate of Tusculum,
  He rushed up the long white street;
He rushed by tower and temple,
  And paused not from his race 530
Till he stood before his master's door
  In the stately market-place.
And straightway round him gathered
  A pale and trembling crowd;
And, when they knew him, cries of rage 535
  Brake forth, and wailing loud;
And women rent their tresses
  For their great prince's fall;
And old men girt on their old swords,
  And went to man the wall. 540

XXX.

But like a graven image
  Black Auster kept his place,
And ever wistfully he looked
  Into his master's face.
The raven mane that daily, 545
  With pats and fond caresses,

The young Herminia washed and combed,
    And twined in even tresses,
And decked with colored ribbons
    From her own gay attire,   550
Hung sadly o'er her father's corpse
    In carnage and in mire.
Forth with a shout sprang Titus
    And seized black Auster's rein.
Then Aulus sware a fearful oath,   555
    And ran at him amain :
"The furies of thy brother
    With me and mine abide,
If one of your accursed house
    Upon black Auster ride!"   560
As on an Alpine watch-tower
    From heaven comes down the flame,
Full on the neck of Titus
    The blade of Aulus came ;
And out the red blood spouted   565
    In a wide arch and tall,
As spouts a fountain in the court
    Of some rich Capuan's hall.
The knees of all the Latines
    Were loosened with dismay   570
When dead, on dead Herminius,
    The bravest Tarquin lay.

XXXI.

And Aulus the Dictator
    Stroked Auster's raven mane ;
With heed he looked unto the girths,   575
    With heed unto the rein :
"Now bear me well, black Auster,
    Into yon thick array,

And thou and I will have revenge
   For thy good lord this day."   580

XXXII.

So spake he, and was buckling
   Tighter black Auster's band,
When he was aware of a princely pair
   That rode at his right hand.
So like they were, no mortal   585
   Might one from other know;
White as snow their armor was,
   Their steeds were white as snow.
Never on earthly anvil
   Did such rare armor gleam,   590
And never did such gallant steeds
   Drink of an earthly stream.

XXXIII.

And all who saw them trembled,
   And pale grew every cheek;
And Aulus the Dictator   595
   Scarce gathered voice to speak:
"Say by what name men call you;
   What city is your home?
And wherefore ride ye in such guise
   Before the ranks of Rome?"   600

XXXIV.

"By many names men call us,
   In many lands we dwell:
Well Samothracia knows us,
   Cyrene knows us well;
Our house in gay Tarentum   605
   Is hung each morn with flowers;

High o'er the masts of Syracuse
   Our marble portal towers;
But by the proud Eurotas
   Is our dear native home;   610
And for the right we come to fight
   Before the ranks of Rome."

XXXV.

So answered those strange horsemen,
   And each couched low his spear;
And forthwith all the ranks of Rome   615
   Were bold and of good cheer;
And on the thirty armies
   Came wonder and affright,
And Ardea wavered on the left,
   And Cora on the right.   620
"Rome to the charge!" cried Aulus,
   "The foe begins to yield!
Charge for the hearth of Vesta!
   Charge for the Golden Shield!
Let no man stop to plunder,   625
   But slay, and slay, and slay;
The Gods who live forever
   Are on our side to-day."

XXXVI.

Then the fierce trumpet-flourish
   From earth to heaven arose.   630
The kites know well the long stern swell
   That bids the Romans close.
Then the good sword of Aulus
   Was lifted up to slay;
Then like a crag down Apennine   635
   Rushed Auster through the fray.

But under those strange horsemen
   Still thicker lay the slain;
And after those strange horses
   Black Auster toiled in vain. 640
Behind them Rome's long battle
   Came rolling on the foe,
Ensigns dancing wild above,
   Blades all in line below.
So comes the Po in flood-time 645
   Upon the Celtic plain;
So comes the squall, blacker than night,
   Upon the Adrian main.
Now, by our Sire Quirinus,
   It was a goodly sight 650
To see the thirty standards
   Swept down the tide of flight.
So flies the spray of Adria
   When the black squall doth blow;
So corn-sheaves in the flood-time 655
   Spin down the whirling Po.
False Sextus to the mountains
   Turned first his horse's head;
And fast fled Ferentinum,
   And fast Lanuvium fled. 660
The horsemen of Nomentum
   Spurred hard out of the fray;
The footmen of Velitræ
   Threw shield and spear away;
And underfoot was trampled, 665
   Amidst the mud and gore,
The banner of proud Tusculum,
   That never stooped before;
And down went Flavius Faustus,
   Who led his stately ranks 670

From where the apple-blossoms wave
   On Anio's echoing banks ;
And Tullus of Arpinum,
   Chief of the Volscian aids,
And Metius with the long fair curls,   675
   The love of Anxur's maids,
And the white head of Vulso,
   The great Arician seer,
And Nepos of Laurentum,
   The hunter of the deer;   680
And in the back false Sextus
   Felt the good Roman steel,
And wriggling in the dust he died
   Like a worm beneath the wheel ;
And fliers and pursuers   685
   Were mingled in a mass ;
And far away the battle
   Went roaring through the pass.

XXXVII

Sempronius Atratinus
   Sat in the Eastern Gate ;   690
Beside him were three Fathers,
   Each in his chair of state —
Fabius, whose nine stout grandsons
   That day were in the field,
And Manlius, eldest of the Twelve   695
   Who kept the Golden Shield,
And Sergius, the High Pontiff,
   For wisdom far renowned ;
In all Etruria's colleges
   Was no such Pontiff found.   700
And all around the portal,
   And high above the wall,

Stood a great throng of people,
   But sad and silent all;
Young lads and stooping elders   705
   That might not bear the mail,
Matrons with lips that quivered,
   And maids with faces pale.
Since the first gleam of daylight,
   Sempronius had not ceased   710
To listen for the rushing
   Of horse-hoofs from the east.
The mist of eve was rising,
   The sun was hastening down,
When he was aware of a princely pair   715
   Fast pricking towards the town.
So like they were, man never
   Saw twins so like before;
Red with gore their armor was,
   Their steeds were red with gore.   720

XXXVIII.

"Hail to the great Asylum!
   Hail to the hill-tops seven!
Hail to the fire that burns for aye,
   And the shield that fell from heaven!
This day, by Lake Regillus,   725
   Under the Porcian height,
All in the lands of Tusculum,
   Was fought a glorious fight.
To-morrow your Dictator
   Shall bring in triumph home   730
The spoils of thirty cities
   To deck the shrines of Rome!"

XXXIX.

Then burst from that great concourse
  A shout that shook the towers,
And some ran north, and some ran south,   735
  Crying, "The day is ours!"
But on rode the strange horsemen
  With slow and lordly pace,
And none who saw their bearing
  Durst ask their name or race.   740
On rode they to the Forum,
  While laurel-boughs and flowers,
From housetops and from windows,
  Fell on their crests in showers.
When they drew nigh to Vesta,   745
  They vaulted down amain,
And washed their horses in the well
  That springs by Vesta's fane.
And straight again they mounted,
  And rode to Vesta's door;   750
Then, like a blast, away they passed,
  And no man saw them more.

XL.

And all the people trembled,
  And pale grew every cheek;
And Sergius the High Pontiff   755
  Alone found voice to speak:
"The Gods who live forever
  Have fought for Rome to-day!
These be the Great Twin Brethren
  To whom the Dorians pray.   760
Back comes the Chief in triumph
  Who in the hour of fight

Hath seen the Great Twin Brethren
    In harness on his right.
Safe comes the ship to haven,
    Through billows and through gales,
If once the Great Twin Brethren
    Sit shining on the sails.
Wherefore they washed their horses
    In Vesta's holy well,
Wherefore they rode to Vesta's door,
    I know, but may not tell.
Here, hard by Vesta's Temple,
    Build we a stately dome
Unto the Great Twin Brethren
    Who fought so well for Rome.
And when the months returning
    Bring back this day of fight,
The proud Ides of Quintilis,
    Marked evermore with white,
Unto the Great Twin Brethren
    Let all the people throng
With chaplets and with offerings,
    With music and with song;
And let the doors and windows
    Be hung with garlands all,
And let the Knights be summoned
    To Mars without the wall;
Thence let them ride in purple
    With joyous trumpet-sound,
Each mounted on his war-horse,
    And each with olive crowned;
And pass in solemn order
    Before the sacred dome
Where dwell the Great Twin Brethren
    Who fought so well for Rome!"

VIRGINIA.

A COLLECTION consisting exclusively of war-songs would give an imperfect, or rather an erroneous, notion of the spirit of the old Latin ballads. The Patricians, during more than a century after the expulsion of the Kings, held all the high military commands. A Plebeian, even though, like Lucius Siccius, he were distinguished by his valor and knowledge of war, could serve only in subordinate posts. A minstrel, therefore, who wished to celebrate the early triumphs of his country, could hardly take any but Patricians for his heroes. The warriors who are mentioned in the two preceding lays, Horatius, Lartius, Herminius, Aulus Posthumius, Æbutius Elva, Sempronius Atratinus, Valerius Poplicola, were all members of the dominant order; and a poet who was singing their praises, whatever his own political opinions might be, would naturally abstain from insulting the class to which they belonged, and from reflecting on the system which had placed such men at the head of the legions of the Commonwealth.

But there was a class of compositions in which the great families were by no means so courteously treated. No parts of early Roman history are richer with poetical coloring than those which relate to the long contest between the privileged houses and the commonalty. The population of Rome was, from a very early period, divided into hereditary castes, which, indeed, readily united to repel foreign enemies, but which regarded each other, during many years, with bitter animosity. Between those castes there was a barrier hardly less strong than that which, at Venice, parted the members of the Great Council from their countrymen. In some respects, indeed, the line which separated an Icilius or a Duilius from a Posthumius or a Fabius was even more deeply marked than that which separated the rower of a gondola from a Contarini or a Morosini. At Venice the distinction was merely civil. At Rome it was both civil and religious. Among the grievances under which the Plebeians suffered, three were felt as peculiarly severe. They were excluded from the highest magistracies; they were excluded from all share in the public lands; and they were ground down to the dust by partial and barbarous legislation touching pecuniary contracts. The ruling class in Rome was a moneyed class; and it made and administered the laws with a view solely to its own interest. Thus the relation between lender and borrower was mixed up with the relation between sovereign and subject. The great men held a large portion of the community in dependence by means of advances at enormous usury. The law of debt, framed by creditors and for the protection of creditors, was the most horrible that has ever been known among men. The liberty and even the life of the insolvent were at the mercy of the Patrician money-lenders. Children often became slaves in consequence of the misfortunes of their parents. The debtor was imprisoned, not in a public gaol under the care of impartial public functionaries, but in a private workhouse belonging to the creditor. Frightful stories were told respecting these dungeons. It was said that torture and brutal violation were common; that tight stocks, heavy chains, scanty measures of food, were used to punish wretches guilty of nothing but poverty; and that brave soldiers, whose breasts were covered with honorable scars, were often marked still more deeply on the back by the scourges of high-born usurers.

The Plebeians were, however, not wholly without constitutional rights. From an early period they had been admitted to some share of political power. They were enrolled each in his century, and were allowed a share, considerable though not proportioned to their numerical strength, in the disposal of those high dignities from which they were themselves excluded. Thus their position bore some resemblance to that of the Irish Catholics during the interval between the year 1792 and the year 1829. The Plebeians had also the privilege of annually appointing officers, named Tribunes, who had no active share in the government of the Commonwealth, but who, by degrees, acquired a power formidable even to the ablest and most resolute Consuls and Dictators. The person of the Tribune was inviolable; and, though he could directly effect little, he could obstruct everything.

During more than a century after the institution of the Tribuneship, the Commons struggled manfully for the removal of the grievances under which they labored; and, in spite of many checks and reverses, succeeded in wringing concession after concession from the stubborn aristocracy. At length, in the year of the city 378, both parties mustered their whole strength for their last and most desperate conflict. The popular and active Tribune, Caius Licinius, proposed the three memorable laws which are called by his name, and which were intended to redress the three great evils of which the Plebeians complained. He was supported with eminent ability and firmness by his colleague, Lucius Sextius. The struggle appears to have been the fiercest that ever in any community terminated without an appeal to arms. If such a contest had raged in any Greek city, the streets would have run with blood. But, even in the paroxysms of faction, the Roman retained his gravity, his respect for law, and his tenderness for the lives of his fellow-citizens. Year after year Licinius and Sextius were re-elected Tribunes. Year after year, if the narrative which has come down to us is to be trusted, they continued to exert, to the full extent, their power of stopping the whole machine of government. No curule magistrates could be chosen ; no military muster could be held. We know too little of the state of Rome in those days to be able to conjecture how, during that long anarchy, the peace was kept and ordinary justice administered between man and man. The animosity of both parties rose to the greatest height. The excitement, we may well suppose, would have been peculiarly intense at the annual election of Tribunes. On such occasions there can be little doubt that the great families did all that could be done, by threats and caresses, to break the union of the Plebeians. That union, however, proved indissoluble. At length the good cause triumphed. The Licinian laws were carried. Lucius Sextius was the first Plebeian Consul, Caius Licinius the third.

The results of this great change were singularly happy and glorious. Two centuries of prosperity, harmony, and victory followed the reconciliation of the orders. Men who remembered Rome engaged in waging petty wars almost within sight of the Capitol lived to see her the mistress of Italy. While the disabilities of the Plebeians continued, she was scarcely able to maintain her ground against the Volscians and Hernicans. When those disabilities were removed, she rapidly became more than a match for Carthage and Macedon.

During the great Licinian contest the Plebeian poets were, doubtless, not silent. Even in modern times songs

have been by no means without influence on public affairs ;
and we may therefore infer that, in a society where printing was unknown and where books were rare, a pathetic
or humorous party-ballad must have produced effects such
as we can but faintly conceive. It is certain that satirical
poems were common at Rome from a very early period.
The rustics, who lived at a distance from the seat of
government, and took little part in the strife of factions,
gave vent to their petty local animosities in coarse Fescen-
nine verse. The lampoons of the city were doubtless of
a higher order; and their sting was early felt by the
nobility. For in the Twelve Tables, long before the time
of the Licinian laws, a severe punishment was denounced
against the citizen who should compose or recite verses
reflecting on another.[1] Satire is, indeed, the only sort of
composition in which the Latin poets whose works have
come down to us were not mere imitators of foreign models ; and it is therefore the only sort of composition in
which they have never been rivalled. It was not, like
their tragedy, their comedy, their epic and lyric poetry, a
hothouse plant which, in return for assiduous and skilful culture, gave only scanty and sickly fruits. It was
hardy and full of sap ; and in all the various juices which
it yielded might be distinguished the flavor of the Ausonian soil. "Satire," says Quinctilian with just pride, " is
all our own." Satire sprang, in truth, naturally from the
constitution of the Roman government and from the spirit
of the Roman people ; and, though at length subjected
to metrical rules derived from Greece, retained to the last

---

[1] Cicero justly infers from this law that there had been early Latin
poets whose works had been lost before his time. ' Quamquam id
quidem etiam xii tabulæ declarant, condi jam tum solitum esse carmen, quod ne liceret fieri ad alterius injuriam lege sanxerunt.' —
Tusc. iv. 2.

an essentially Roman character. Lucilius was the earliest satirist whose works were held in esteem under the Cæsars. But, many years before Lucilius was born, Nævius had been flung into a dungeon and guarded there with circumstances of unusual rigor, on account of the bitter lines in which he had attacked the great Cæcilian family.[1] The genius and spirit of the Roman satirist survived the liberty of their country, and were not extinguished by the cruel despotism of the Julian and Flavian Emperors. The great poet who told the story of Domitian's turbot was the legitimate successor of those forgotten minstrels whose songs animated the factions of the infant Republic.

These minstrels, as Niebuhr has remarked, appear to have generally taken the popular side. We can hardly be mistaken in supposing that, at the great crisis of the civil conflict, they employed themselves in versifying all the most powerful and virulent speeches of the Tribunes, and in heaping abuse on the leaders of the aristocracy. Every personal defect, every domestic scandal, every tradition dishonorable to a noble house, would be sought out, brought into notice, and exaggerated. The illustrious head of the aristocratical party, Marcus Furius Camillus, might perhaps be, in some measure, protected by his venerable age and by the memory of his great services to the State. But Appius Claudius Crassus enjoyed no such immunity. He was descended from a long line of ancestors distinguished by their haughty demeanor, and by the inflexibility with which they had withstood all the demands of the Plebeian order. While the political conduct and the deportment of the Claudian nobles drew upon them the fiercest public hatred, they were accused of wanting, if any credit is due to the early history of Rome, a class of qualities which, in the military commonwealth, is suf-

---

[1] Plautus, *Miles Gloriosus*. Aulus Gellius, iii. 3.

ficient to cover a multitude of offences. The chiefs of
the family appear to have been eloquent, versed in civil
business, and learned after the fashion of their age; but
in war they were not distinguished by skill or valor.
Some of them, as if conscious where their weakness lay,
had, when filling the highest magistracies, taken internal
administration as their department of public business,
and left the military command to their colleagues.[1] One
of them had been intrusted with an army, and had failed
ignominiously.[2] None of them had been honored with a
triumph. None of them had achieved any martial exploit,
such as those by which Lucius Quinctius Cincinnatus,
Titus Quinctius Capitolinus, Aulus Cornelius Cossus,
and, above all, the great Camillus, had extorted the re-
luctant esteem of the multitude. During the Licinian
conflict, Appius Claudius Crassus signalized himself by
the ability and severity with which he harangued against
the two great agitators. He would naturally, therefore,
be the favorite mark of the Plebeian satirists; nor would
they have been at a loss to find a point on which he was
open to attack.

His grandfather, called, like himself, Appius Claudius,
had left a name as much detested as that of Sextus Tarquinius. This elder Appius had been Consul more than
seventy years before the introduction of the Licinian laws.
By availing himself of a singular crisis in public feeling,
he had obtained the consent of the Commons to the
abolition of the Tribuneship, and had been the chief of
that Council of Ten to which the whole direction of the
State had been committed. In a few months his administration had become universally odious. It had been
swept away by an irresistible outbreak of popular fury;

---
[1] In the years of the city 260, 304, 330.
[2] In the year of the city 282.

and its memory was still held in abhorrence by the whole city. The immediate cause of the downfall of this execrable government was said to have been an attempt made by Appius Claudius upon the chastity of a beautiful young girl of humble birth. The story ran that the Decemvir, unable to succeed by bribes and solicitations, resorted to an outrageous act of tyranny. A vile dependant of the Claudian house laid claim to the damsel as his slave. The cause was brought before the tribunal of Appius. The wicked magistrate, in defiance of the clearest proofs, gave judgment for the claimant. But the girl's father, a brave soldier, saved her from servitude and dishonor by stabbing her to the heart in the sight of the whole Forum. That blow was the signal for a general explosion. Camp and city rose at once; the Ten were pulled down; the Tribuneship was re-established; and Appius escaped the hands of the executioner only by a voluntary death.

It can hardly be doubted that a story so admirably adapted to the purposes both of the poet and of the demagogue would be eagerly seized upon by minstrels burning with hatred against the Patrician order, against the Claudian house, and especially against the grandson and namesake of the infamous Decemvir.

In order that the reader may judge fairly of these fragments of the lay of Virginia, he must imagine himself a Plebeian who has just voted for the re-election of Sextius and Licinius. All the power of the Patricians has been exerted to throw out the two great champions of the Commons. Every Posthumius, Æmilius, and Cornelius has used his influence to the utmost. Debtors have been let out of the workhouses on condition of voting against the men of the people; clients have been posted to hiss and interrupt the favorite candidates; Appius Claudius Crassus has spoken with more than his usual eloquence

and asperity; all has been in vain; Licinius and Sextius
have a fifth time carried all the tribes; work is suspended;
the booths are closed; the Plebeians bear on their shoulders the two champions of liberty through the Forum.
Just at this moment it is announced that a popular poet,
a zealous adherent of the Tribunes, has made a new song
which will cut the Claudian nobles to the heart. The
crowd gathers round him and calls on him to recite it.
He takes his stand on the spot where, according to tradition, Virginia, more than seventy years ago, was seized
by the pander of Appius, and he begins his story.

VIRGINIA.

FRAGMENTS OF A LAY SUNG IN THE FORUM ON THE DAY
WHEREON LUCIUS SEXTIUS SEXTINUS LATERANUS AND
CAIUS LICINIUS CALVUS STOLO WERE ELECTED TRI-
BUNES OF THE COMMONS THE FIFTH TIME, IN THE
YEAR OF THE CITY CCCLXXXII.

YE good men of the Commons, with loving hearts and
    true,
Who stand by the bold Tribunes that still have stood by
    you,
Come, make a circle round me, and mark my tale with
    care, —
A tale of what Rome once hath borne, of what Rome yet
    may bear.
This is no Grecian fable, of fountains running wine,
Of maids with snaky tresses, or sailors turned to swine.
Here, in this very Forum, under the noonday sun,

In sight of all the people, the bloody deed was done.
Old men still creep among us who saw that fearful day,
Just seventy years and seven ago, when the wicked Ten
    bare sway.

Of all the wicked Ten still the names are held accursed,
And of all the wicked Ten Appius Claudius was the worst.
He stalked along the Forum like King Tarquin in his
    pride;
Twelve axes waited on him, six marching on a side.
The townsmen shrank to right and left, and eyed as-
    kance with fear
His lowering brow, his curling mouth, which always
    seemed to sneer.
That brow of hate, that mouth of scorn, marks all the
    kindred still;
For never was there Claudius yet but wished the Com-
    mons ill.
Nor lacks he fit attendance; for close behind his heels,
With outstretched chin and crouching pace, the client
    Marcus steals,
His loins girt up to run with speed, be the errand what
    it may,
And the smile flickering on his cheek for aught his lord
    may say.
Such varlets pimp and jest for hire among the lying
    Greeks;
Such varlets still are paid to hoot when brave Licinius
    speaks.
Where'er ye shed the honey, the buzzing flies will crowd;
Where'er ye fling the carrion, the raven's croak is loud;
Where'er down Tiber garbage floats, the greedy pike ye
    see;
And wheresoe'er such lord is found, such client still will be.

Just then, as through one cloudless chink in a black
    stormy sky
Shines out the dewy morning-star, a fair young girl came
    by.   30
With her small tablets in her hand and her satchel on her
    arm,
Home she went bounding from the school, nor dreamed of
    shame or harm;
And past those dreaded axes she innocently ran,
With bright, frank brow that had not learned to blush at
    gaze of man;
And up the Sacred Street she turned, and, as she danced
    along,   35
She warbled gaily to herself lines of the good old song,
How for a sport the princes came spurring from the camp,
And found Lucrece combing the fleece under the midnight
    lamp.
The maiden sang as sings the lark, when up he darts his
    flight
From his nest in the green April corn to meet the morn-
    ing light;   40
And Appius heard her sweet young voice, and saw her
    sweet young face,
And loved her with the accursed love of his accursed race,
And all along the Forum and up the Sacred Street
His vulture eye pursued the trip of those small glancing
    feet.

        *   *   *   *   *   *   *   *

Over the Alban mountains the light of morning broke; 45
From all the roofs of the Seven Hills curled the thin
    wreaths of smoke;
The city-gates were opened; the Forum, all alive
With buyers and with sellers, was humming like a hive;

Blithely on brass and timber the craftsman's stroke was ringing,
And blithely o'er her panniers the market-girl was singing, 50
And blithely young Virginia came smiling from her home;
Ah! woe for young Virginia, the sweetest maid in Rome!
With her small tablets in her hand and her satchel on her arm,
Forth she went bounding to the school, nor dreamed of shame or harm.
She crossed the Forum shining with stalls in alleys gay, 55
And just had reached the very spot whereon I stand this day,
When up the varlet Marcus came; not such as when erewhile
He crouched behind his patron's heels with the true client smile;
He came with lowering forehead, swollen features, and clenched fist,
And strode across Virginia's path, and caught her by the wrist. 60
Hard strove the frighted maiden and screamed with look aghast,
And at her scream from right and left the folk came running fast, —
The money-changer Crispus, with his thin silver hairs,
And Hanno from the stately booth glittering with Punic wares,
And the strong smith Murœna, grasping a half-forged brand, 65
And Volero the flesher, his cleaver in his hand.
All came in wrath and wonder, for all knew that fair child,
And, as she passed them twice a day, all kissed their hands and smiled;
And the strong smith Murœna gave Marcus such a blow,

The caitiff reeled three paces back, and let the maiden go. 70
Yet glared he fiercely round him, and growled in harsh, fell tone,
" She's mine, and I will have her; I seek but for mine own.
She is my slave, born in my house, and stolen away and sold,
The year of the sore sickness, ere she was twelve hours old.
'T was in the sad September, the month of wail and fright; 75
Two augurs were borne forth that morn, the Consul died ere night.
I wait on Appius Claudius, I waited on his sire;
Let him who works the client wrong beware the patron's ire!"

So spake the varlet Marcus; and dread and silence came
On all the people at the sound of the great Claudian name. 80
For then there was no Tribune to speak the word of might,
Which makes the rich man tremble, and guards the poor man's right.
There was no brave Licinius, no honest Sextius then;
But all the city in great fear obeyed the wicked Ten.
Yet ere the varlet Marcus again might seize the maid, 85
Who clung tight to Muræna's skirt and sobbed and shrieked for aid,
Forth through the throng of gazers the young Icilius pressed,
And stamped his foot, and rent his gown, and smote upon his breast,
And sprang upon that column, by many a minstrel sung,
Whereon three mouldering helmets, three rusting swords, are hung, 90
And beckoned to the people, and in bold voice and clear
Poured thick and fast the burning words which tyrants quake to hear:

"Now, by your children's cradles, now by your fathers'
    graves,
Be men to-day, Quirites, or be forever slaves!
For this did Servius give us laws? For this did Lucrece
    bleed?
For this was the great vengeance wrought on Tarquin's
    evil seed?
For this did those false sons make red the axes of their sire?
For this did Scævola's right hand hiss in the Tuscan fire?
Shall the vile fox-earth awe the race that stormed the
    lion's den?
Shall we, who could not brook one lord, crouch to the
    wicked Ten?
O for that ancient spirit which curbed the Senate's will!
O for the tents which in old time whitened the Sacred Hill!
In those brave days our fathers stood firmly side by side;
They faced the Marcian fury, they tamed the Fabian pride;
They drove the fiercest Quinctius an outcast forth from
    Rome;
They sent the haughtiest Claudius with shivered fasces
    home.
But what their care bequeathed us our madness flung away;
All the ripe fruit of threescore years was blighted in a day.
Exult, ye proud Patricians! The hard-fought fight is o'er.
We strove for honors — 't was in vain; for freedom —
    't is no more.
No crier to the polling summons the eager throng;
No Tribune breathes the word of might that guards the
    weak from wrong.
Our very hearts, that were so high, sink down beneath your
    will.
Riches and lands, and power and state — ye have them;
    keep them still.
Still keep the holy fillets; still keep the purple gown,

The axes and the curule chair, the car and laurel crown;
Still press us for your cohorts, and, when the fight is done,
Still fill your garners from the soil which our good swords
    have won.
Still, like a spreading ulcer which leech-craft may not cure,
Let your foul usance eat away the substance of the poor. 120
Still let your haggard debtors bear all their fathers bore;
Still let your dens of torment be noisome as of yore;
No fire when Tiber freezes, no air in dog-star heat;
And store of rods for free-born backs, and holes for free-
    born feet.
Heap heavier still the fetters, bar closer still the grate; 125
Patient as sheep we yield us up unto your cruel hate.
But, by the Shades beneath us, and by the Gods above,
Add not unto your cruel hate your yet more cruel love!
Have ye not graceful ladies, whose spotless lineage springs
From Consuls and High Pontiffs and ancient Alban
    kings — 130
Ladies who deign not on our paths to set their tender feet,
Who from their cars look down with scorn upon the won-
    dering street,
Who in Corinthian mirrors their own proud smiles behold,
And breathe of Capuan odors, and shine with Spanish
    gold?
Then leave the poor Plebeian his single tie to life — 135
The sweet, sweet love of daughter, of sister, and of wife,
The gentle speech, the balm for all that his vexed soul
    endures,
The kiss, in which he half forgets even such a yoke as
    yours.
Still let the maiden's beauty swell the father's breast with
    pride;
Still let the bridegroom's arms infold an unpolluted bride. 140
Spare us the inexpiable wrong, the unutterable shame,

That turns the coward's heart to steel, the sluggard's blood
 to flame,
Lest, when our latest hope is fled, ye taste of our despair,
And learn by proof in some wild hour how much the
 wretched dare."

* * * * * * * *
* * * * * * * *

Straightway Virginius led the maid a little space aside,   145
To where the reeking shambles stood, piled up with horn
 and hide,
Close to yon low dark archway, where in a crimson flood
Leaps down to the great sewer the gurgling stream of
 blood.
Hard by, a flesher on a block had laid his whittle down;
Virginius caught the whittle up and hid it in his gown.   150
And then his eyes grew very dim, and his throat began to
 swell,
And in a hoarse, changed voice he spake, "Farewell, sweet
 child! Farewell!
O, how I loved my darling! Though stern I sometimes be,
To thee thou know'st I was not so. Who could be so to
 thee?
And how my darling loved me! How glad she was to hear 155
My footstep on the threshold when I came back last year!
And how she danced with pleasure to see my civic crown,
And took my sword and hung it up, and brought me forth
 my gown!
Now, all those things are over—yes, all thy pretty ways,
Thy needlework, thy prattle, thy snatches of old lays;   160
And none will grieve when I go forth, or smile when I
 return,
Or watch beside the old man's bed, or weep upon his urn.
The house that was the happiest within the Roman walls,

The house that envied not the wealth of Capua's marble
    halls,
Now, for the brightness of thy smile, must have eternal
    gloom, 165
And for the music of thy voice, the silence of the tomb.
The time is come. See how he points his eager hand this
    way!
See how his eyes gloat on thy grief like a kite's upon the
    prey!
With all his wit, he little deems that, spurned, betrayed,
    bereft,
Thy father hath in his despair one fearful refuge left. 170
He little deems that in this hand I clutch what still can save
Thy gentle youth from taunts and blows, the portion of the
    slave;
Yea, and from nameless evil, that passeth taunt and blow —
Foul outrage which thou knowest not, which thou shalt
    never know.
Then clasp me round the neck once more, and give me
    one more kiss; 175
And now, mine own dear little girl, there is no way but
    this."
With that he lifted high the steel and smote her in the side,
And in her blood she sank to earth, and with one sob she
    died.

Then, for a little moment, all people held their breath,
And through the crowded Forum was stillness as of death; 180
And in another moment brake forth from one and all
A cry as if the Volscians were coming o'er the wall.
Some with averted faces shrieking fled home amain;
Some ran to call a leech, and some ran to lift the slain;
Some felt her lips and little wrist, if life might there be
    found; 185

And some tore up their garments fast, and strove to stanch the wound.
In vain they ran and felt and stanched; for never truer blow
That good right arm had dealt in fight against a Volscian foe.

  When Appius Claudius saw that deed, he shuddered and sank down,
And hid his face some little space with the corner of his gown, 190
Till with white lips and bloodshot eyes Virginius tottered nigh,
And stood before the judgment-seat, and held the knife on high.
"O dwellers in the nether gloom, avengers of the slain,
By this dear blood I cry to you, do right between us twain:
And even as Appius Claudius hath dealt by me and mine, 195
Deal you by Appius Claudius and all the Claudian line!"
So spake the slayer of his child, and turned and went his way;
But first he cast one haggard glance to where the body lay,
And writhed, and groaned a fearful groan, and then with steadfast feet
Strode right across the market-place unto the Sacred Street. 200

  Then up sprang Appius Claudius: "Stop him, alive or dead!
Ten thousand pounds of copper to the man who brings his head."
He looked upon his clients, but none would work his will;

He looked upon his lictors, but they trembled and stood still.
And, as Virginius through the press his way in silence cleft, 205
Ever the mighty multitude fell back to right and left.
And he hath passed in safety unto his woful home,
And there ta'en horse to tell the camp what deeds are done in Rome.

By this the flood of people was swollen from every side,
And streets and porches round were filled with that o'er-flowing tide; 210
And close around the body gathered a little train
Of them that were the nearest and dearest to the slain.
They brought a bier, and hung it with many a cypress crown,
And gently they uplifted her, and gently laid her down.
The face of Appius Claudius wore the Claudian scowl and sneer, 215
And in the Claudian note he cried, "What doth this rabble here?
Have they no crafts to mind at home, that hitherward they stray?
Ho! lictors, clear the market-place, and fetch the corpse away!"
The voice of grief and fury till then had not been loud;
But a deep sullen murmur wandered among the crowd, 220
Like the moaning noise that goes before the whirlwind on the deep,
Or the growl of a fierce watch-dog but half aroused from sleep.
But when the lictors at that word, tall yeomen all and strong,
Each with his axe and sheaf of twigs, went down into the throng,

Those old men say who saw that day of sorrow and of
    sin 225
That in the Roman Forum was never such a din.
The wailing, hooting, cursing, the howls of grief and hate,
Were heard beyond the Pincian Hill, beyond the Latin
    Gate.
But close around the body, where stood the little train
Of them that were the nearest and dearest to the slain, 230
No cries were there, but teeth set fast, low whispers and
    black frowns,
And breaking up of benches and girding up of gowns.
'T was well the lictors might not pierce to where the
    maiden lay,
Else surely had they been all twelve torn limb from limb
    that day.
Right glad they were to struggle back, blood streaming
    from their heads, 235
With axes all in splinters and raiment all in shreds.
Then Appius Claudius gnawed his lip, and the blood left
    his cheek,
And thrice he beckoned with his hand, and thrice he strove
    to speak;
And thrice the tossing Forum set up a frightful yell:
"See, see, thou dog! what thou hast done, and hide thy
    shame in hell! 240
Thou that wouldst make our maidens slaves must first
    make slaves of men.
Tribunes! Hurrah for Tribunes! Down with the wicked
    Ten!"
And straightway, thick as hailstones, came whizzing
    through the air
Pebbles and bricks and potsherds all round the curule
    chair;
And upon Appius Claudius great fear and trembling came, 245

For never was a Claudius yet brave against aught but
    shame.
Though the great houses love us not, we own, to do them
    right,
That the great houses, all save one, have borne them well
    in fight.
Still Caius of Corioli, his triumphs and his wrongs,
His vengeance and his mercy, live in our camp-fire songs. 250
Beneath the yoke of Furius oft have Gaul and Tuscan
    bowed;
And Rome may bear the pride of him of whom herself is
    proud.
But evermore a Claudius shrinks from a stricken field,
And changes color like a maid at sight of sword and
    shield.
The Claudian triumphs all were won within the city
    towers;   255
The Claudian yoke was never pressed on any necks but
    ours.
A Cossus, like a wild cat, springs ever at the face;
A Fabius rushes like a boar against the shouting chase;
But the vile Claudian litter, raging with currish spite,
Still yelps and snaps at those who run, still runs from
    those who smite.   260
So now 't was seen of Appius; when stones began to fly,
He shook and crouched, and wrung his hands, and smote
    upon his thigh:
"Kind clients, honest lictors, stand by me in this fray!
Must I be torn in pieces? Home, home, the nearest
    way!"
While yet he spake, and looked around with a bewildered
    stare,   265
Four sturdy lictors put their necks beneath the curule
    chair;

And fourscore clients on the left and fourscore on the right
Arrayed themselves with swords and staves, and loins girt
    up for fight.
But, though without or staff or sword, so furious was the
    throng
That scarce the train with might and main could bring
    their lord along.   270
Twelve times the crowd made at him, five times they
    seized his gown;
Small chance was his to rise again, if once they got him
    down;
And sharper came the pelting, and evermore the yell —
"Tribunes! we will have Tribunes!"— rose with a louder
    swell;
And the chair tossed as tosses a bark with tattered sail   275
When raves the Adriatic beneath an eastern gale,
When the Calabrian sea-marks are lost in clouds of spume,
And the great Thunder-Cape has donned his veil of inky
    gloom.
One stone hit Appius in the mouth, and one beneath the
    ear,
And ere he reached Mount Palatine he swooned with
    pain and fear.   280
His cursed head, that he was wont to hold so high with
    pride,
Now, like a drunken man's, hung down and swayed from
    side to side;
And when his stout retainers had brought him to his door,
His face and neck were all one cake of filth and clotted
    gore.
As Appius Claudius was that day, so may his grandson be!
God send Rome one such other sight, and send me there
    to see!   286

THE PROPHECY OF CAPYS.

It can hardly be necessary to remind any reader that, according to the popular tradition, Romulus, after he had slain his grand-uncle Amulius, and restored his grandfather Numitor, determined to quit Alba, the hereditary domain of the Sylvian princes, and to found a new city. The Gods, it was added, vouchsafed the clearest signs of the favor with which they regarded the enterprise, and of the high destinies reserved for the young colony.

This event was likely to be a favorite theme of the old Latin minstrels. They would naturally attribute the project of Romulus to some divine intimation of the power and prosperity which it was decreed that his city should attain. They would probably introduce seers foretelling the victories of unborn Consuls and Dictators, and the last great victory would generally occupy the most conspicuous place in the prediction. There is nothing strange in the supposition that the poet who was employed to celebrate the first great triumph of the Romans over the Greeks might throw his song of exultation into this form.

The occasion was one likely to excite the strongest feelings of national pride. A great outrage had been followed by a great retribution. Seven years before this time, Lucius Posthumius Megellus, who sprang from one of the noblest houses of Rome, and had been thrice Consul, was sent ambassador to Tarentum, with charge to demand reparation for grievous injuries. The Tarentines gave him audience in their theatre, where he addressed them in such Greek as he could command, which, we may well believe, was not exactly such as Cineas would have spoken. An exquisite sense of the ridiculous belonged to the Greek character; and closely connected with this faculty was a strong propensity to flippancy and impertinence. When Posthumius placed an accent wrong, his hearers burst into a laugh. When he remonstrated, they hooted him and called him barbarian, and at length hissed him off the stage as if he had been a bad actor. As the grave Roman retired, a buffoon, who from his constant drunkenness was nicknamed the Pint-pot, came up with gestures of the grossest indecency, and bespattered the senatorial gown with filth. Posthumius turned round to the multitude, and held up the gown, as if appealing to the universal law of nations. The sight only increased the insolence of the Tarentines. They clapped their hands, and set up a shout of laughter which shook the theatre. "Men of Tarentum," said Posthumius, " it will take not a little blood to wash this gown."[1]

Rome, in consequence of this insult, declared war against the Tarentines. The Tarentines sought for allies beyond the Ionian Sea. Pyrrhus, king of Epirus, came to their help with a large army; and, for the first time, the two great nations of antiquity were fairly matched against each other.

The fame of Greece in arms as well as in arts was then at the height. Half a century earlier, the career of Alexander had excited the admiration and terror of all nations from the Ganges to the Pillars of Hercules. Royal houses, founded by Macedonian captains, still reigned at Antioch and Alexandria. That barbarian warriors, led by barbarian chiefs, should win a pitched battle against Greek valor guided by Greek science,

[1] Dion. Hal. *De Legationibus.*

seemed as incredible as it would now seem that the Burmese or the Siamese should, in the open plain, put to flight an equal number of the best English troops. The Tarentines were convinced that their countrymen were irresistible in war; and this conviction had emboldened them to treat with the grossest indignity one whom they regarded as the representative of an inferior race. Of the Greek generals then living, Pyrrhus was indisputably the first. Among the troops who were trained in the Greek discipline his Epirotes ranked high. His expedition to Italy was a turning-point in the history of the world. He found there a people who, far inferior to the Athenians and Corinthians in the fine arts, in the speculative sciences, and in all the refinements of life, were the best soldiers on the face of the earth. Their arms, their gradations of rank, their order of battle, their method of intrenchment, were all of Latian origin, and had all been gradually brought near to perfection, not by the study of foreign models, but by the genius and experience of many generations of great native commanders. The first words which broke from the king, when his practised eye had surveyed the Roman encampment, were full of meaning: "These barbarians," he said, "have nothing barbarous in their military arrangements." He was at first victorious; for his own talents were superior to those of the captains who were opposed to him; and the Romans were not prepared for the onset of the elephants of the East, which were then for the first time seen in Italy — moving mountains, with long snakes for hands.[1] But the victories of the Epirotes were fiercely disputed, dearly purchased, and altogether unprofitable. At length Manius Curius Dentatus, who had in his first

[1] *Anguimanus* is the old Latin epithet for an elephant. Lucretius, ii. 538, v. 1302.

Consulship won two triumphs, was again placed at the head of the Roman Commonwealth, and sent to encounter the invaders. A great battle was fought near Beneventum. Pyrrhus was completely defeated. He repassed the sea; and the world learned with amazement that a people had been discovered who, in fair fighting, were superior to the best troops that had been drilled on the system of Parmenio and Antigonus.

The conquerors had a good right to exult in their success; for their glory was all their own. They had not learned from their enemy how to conquer him. It was with their own national arms, and in their own national battle-array, that they had overcome weapons and tactics long believed to be invincible. The pilum and the broadsword had vanquished the Macedonian spear. The legion had broken the Macedonian phalanx. Even the elephants, when the surprise produced by their first appearance was over, could cause no disorder in the steady yet flexible battalions of Rome.

It is said by Florus, and may easily be believed, that the triumph far surpassed in magnificence any that Rome had previously seen. The only spoils which Papirius Cursor and Fabius Maximus could exhibit were flocks and herds, wagons of rude structure, and heaps of spears and helmets. But now, for the first time, the riches of Asia and the arts of Greece adorned a Roman pageant. Plate, fine stuffs, costly furniture, rare animals, exquisite paintings and sculptures, formed part of the procession. At the banquet would be assembled a crowd of warriors and statesmen, among whom Manius Curius Dentatus would take the highest room. Caius Fabricius Luscinus, then, after two Consulships and two triumphs, Censor of the Commonwealth, would doubtless occupy a place of honor at the board. In situations less conspicuous

probably lay some of those who were, a few years later,
the terror of Carthage, — Caius Duilius, the founder of the
maritime greatness of his country ; Marcus Atilius Regulus, who owed to defeat a renown far higher than that
which he had derived from his victories; and Caius Lutatius Catulus, who, while suffering from a grievous wound,
fought the great battle of the Ægates, and brought the
First Punic War to a triumphant close. It is impossible
to recount the names of these eminent citizens without
reflecting that they were all, without exception, Plebeians,
and would, but for the ever-memorable struggle maintained by Caius Licinius and Lucius Sextius, have been
doomed to hide in obscurity, or to waste in civil broils
the capacity and energy which prevailed against Pyrrhus
and Hamilcar.

On such a day we may suppose that the patriotic enthusiasm of a Latin poet would vent itself in reiterated
shouts of *Io triumphe*, such as were uttered by Horace on
a far less exciting occasion, and in boasts resembling
those which Virgil put into the mouth of Anchises. The
superiority of some foreign nations, and especially of the
Greeks, in the lazy arts of peace would be admitted with
disdainful candor; but pre-eminence in all the qualities
which fit a people to subdue and govern mankind would
be claimed for the Romans.

The following lay belongs to the latest age of Latin
ballad-poetry. Nævius and Livius Andronicus were
probably among the children whose mothers held them
up to see the chariot of Curius go by. The minstrel who
sang on that day might possibly have lived to read the
first hexameters of Ennius, and to see the first comedies
of Plautus. His poem, as might be expected, shows a
much wider acquaintance with the geography, manners,
and productions of remote nations than would have been

found in compositions of the age of Camillus. But he troubles himself little about dates, and having heard travellers talk with admiration of the Colossus of Rhodes, and of the structures and gardens with which the Macedonian kings of Syria had embellished their residence on the banks of the Orontes, he has never thought of inquiring whether these things existed in the age of Romulus.

THE PROPHECY OF CAPYS.

A LAY SUNG AT THE BANQUET IN THE CAPITOL, ON THE DAY WHEREON MANIUS CURIUS DENTATUS, A SECOND TIME CONSUL, TRIUMPHED OVER KING PYRRHUS AND THE TARENTINES, IN THE YEAR OF THE CITY CCCCLXXIX.

I.

Now slain is King Amulius
   Of the great Sylvian line,
Who reigned in Alba Longa
   On the throne of Aventine.
Slain is the Pontiff Camers,
   Who spake the words of doom:
"The children to the Tiber,
   The mother to the tomb."

II.

In Alba's lake no fisher
   His net to-day is flinging;
On the dark rind of Alba's oaks
   To-day no axe is ringing:

The yoke hangs o'er the manger,
  The scythe lies in the hay;
Through all the Alban villages
  No work is done to-day.

III.

And every Alban burgher
  Hath donned his whitest gown;
And every head in Alba
  Weareth a poplar crown;
And every Alban door-post
  With boughs and flowers is gay;
For to-day the dead are living,
  The lost are found to-day.

IV.

They were doomed by a bloody king,
  They were doomed by a lying priest;
They were cast on the raging flood,
  They were tracked by the raging beast.
Raging beast and raging flood
  Alike have spared the prey;
And to-day the dead are living,
  The lost are found to-day.

V.

The troubled river knew them,
  And smoothed his yellow foam,
And gently rocked the cradle
  That bore the fate of Rome.
The ravening she-wolf knew them,
  And licked them o'er and o'er,
And gave them of her own fierce milk,
  Rich with raw flesh and gore.

Twenty winters, twenty springs,
    Since then have rolled away;
And to-day the dead are living,
    The lost are found to-day.

VI.

Blithe it was to see the twins,   45
    Right goodly youths and tall,
Marching from Alba Longa
    To their old grandsire's hall.
Along their path fresh garlands
    Are hung from tree to tree;   50
Before them stride the pipers,
    Piping a note of glee.

VII.

On the right goes Romulus,
    With arms to the elbows red,
And in his hand a broadsword,   55
    And on the blade a head —
A head in an iron helmet,
    With horse-hair hanging down,
A shaggy head, a swarthy head,
    Fixed in a ghastly frown —   60
The head of King Amulius
    Of the great Sylvian line,
Who reigned in Alba Longa
    On the throne of Aventine.

VIII.

On the left side goes Remus,   65
    With wrists and fingers red,
And in his hand a boar-spear,
    And on the point a head —

A wrinkled head and aged,
  With silver beard and hair,   70
And holy fillets round it
  Such as the pontiffs wear —
The head of ancient Camers,
  Who spake the words of doom :
"The children to the Tiber,   75
  The mother to the tomb."

IX.

Two and two behind the twins
  Their trusty comrades go,
Four and forty valiant men,
  With club and axe and bow.   80
On each side every hamlet
  Pours forth its joyous crowd,
Shouting lads and baying dogs
  And children laughing loud,
And old men weeping fondly   85
  As Rhea's boys go by,
And maids who shriek to see the heads,
  Yet, shrieking, press more nigh.

X.

So they marched along the lake ;
  They marched by fold and stall,   90
By corn-field and by vineyard,
  Unto the old man's hall.

XI.

In the hall-gate sat Capys,
  Capys, the sightless seer ;
From head to foot he trembled   95
  As Romulus drew near.

And up stood stiff his thin white hair,
   And his blind eyes flashed fire:
"Hail! foster child of the wondrous nurse!
   Hail! son of the wondrous sire!   100

XII.

"But thou — what dost thou here
   In the old man's peaceful hall?
What doth the eagle in the coop,
   The bison in the stall?
Our corn fills many a garner,   105
   Our vines clasp many a tree,
Our flocks are white on many a hill,
   But these are not for thee.

XIII.

"For thee no treasure ripens
   In the Tartessian mine;   110
For thee no ship brings precious bales
   Across the Libyan brine;
Thou shalt not drink from amber,
   Thou shalt not rest on down;
Arabia shall not steep thy locks,   115
   Nor Sidon tinge thy gown.

XIV.

"Leave gold and myrrh and jewels,
   Rich table and soft bed,
To them who of man's seed are born,
   Whom woman's milk hath fed.   120
Thou wast not made for lucre,
   For pleasure, nor for rest;
Thou, that art sprung from the War-god's loins,
   And hast tugged at the she-wolf's breast.

XV.

"From sunrise unto sunset   125
  All earth shall hear thy fame;
A glorious city thou shalt build,
  And name it by thy name;
And there, unquenched through ages,
  Like Vesta's sacred fire,   130
Shall live the spirit of thy nurse,
  The spirit of thy sire.

XVI.

"The ox toils through the furrow,
  Obedient to the goad;
The patient ass up flinty paths   135
  Plods with his weary load;
With whine and bound the spaniel
  His master's whistle hears;
And the sheep yields her patiently
  To the loud clashing shears.   140

XVII.

"But thy nurse will hear no master,
  Thy nurse will bear no load;
And woe to them that shear her,
  And woe to them that goad!
When all the pack, loud baying,   145
  Her bloody lair surrounds,
She dies in silence, biting hard,
  Amidst the dying hounds.

XVIII.

"Pomona loves the orchard,
  And Liber loves the vine.   150

And Pales loves the straw-built shed
    Warm with the breath of kine;
And Venus loves the whispers
    Of plighted youth and maid,
In April's ivory moonlight   155
    Beneath the chestnut shade.

XIX.

" But thy father loves the clashing
    Of broadsword and of shield;
He loves to drink the steam that reeks
    From the fresh battlefield;   160
He smiles a smile more dreadful
    Than his own dreadful frown,
When he sees the thick black cloud of smoke
    Go up from the conquered town.

XX.

" And such as is the War-god,   165
    The author of thy line,
And such as she who suckled thee,
    Even such be thou and thine.
Leave to the soft Campanian
    His baths and his perfumes;   170
Leave to the sordid race of Tyre
    Their dyeing-vats and looms;
Leave to the sons of Carthage
    The rudder and the oar;
Leave to the Greek his marble Nymphs   175
    And scrolls of wordy lore.

XXI.

" Thine, Roman, is the pilum;
    Roman, the sword is thine,

The even trench, the bristling mound,
    The legion's ordered line;
And thine the wheels of triumph,
    Which with their laurelled train
Move slowly up the shouting streets
    To Jove's eternal fane.

XXII.

"Beneath thy yoke the Volscian
    Shall vail his lofty brow;
Soft Capua's curled revellers
    Before thy chairs shall bow;
The Lucumoes of Arnus
    Shall quake thy rods to see;
And the proud Samnite's heart of steel
    Shall yield to only thee.

XXIII.

"The Gaul shall come against thee
    From the land of snow and night;
Thou shalt give his fair-haired armies
    To the raven and the kite.

XXIV.

"The Greek shall come against thee,
    The conqueror of the East.
Beside him stalks to battle
    The huge earth-shaking beast —
The beast on whom the castle
    With all its guards doth stand,
The beast who hath between his eyes
    The serpent for a hand.
First march the bold Epirotes,
    Wedged close with shield and spear,

And the ranks of false Tarentum
    Are glittering in the rear.

XXV.

"The ranks of false Tarentum
    Like hunted sheep shall fly;   210
In vain the bold Epirotes
    Shall round their standards die;
And Apennine's gray vultures
    Shall have a noble feast
On the fat and the eyes   215
    Of the huge earth-shaking beast.

XXVI.

"Hurrah for the good weapons
    That keep the War-god's land!
Hurrah for Rome's stout pilum
    In a stout Roman hand!   220
Hurrah for Rome's short broadsword,
    That through the thick array
Of levelled spears and serried shields
    Hews deep its gory way!

XXVII.

"Hurrah for the great triumph   225
    That stretches many a mile!
Hurrah for the wan captives
    That pass in endless file!
Ho! bold Epirotes, whither
    Hath the Red King ta'en flight?   230
Ho! dogs of false Tarentum,
    Is not the gown washed white?

XXVIII.

"Hurrah for the great triumph
  That stretches many a mile!
Hurrah for the rich dye of Tyre,   235
  And the fine web of Nile,
The helmets gay with plumage
  Torn from the pheasant's wings,
The belts set thick with starry gems
  That shone on Indian kings,   240
The urns of massy silver,
  The goblets rough with gold,
The many-colored tablets bright
  With loves and wars of old,
The stone that breathes and struggles,   245
  The brass that seems to speak!—
Such cunning they who dwell on high
  Have given unto the Greek.

XXIX.

"Hurrah for Manius Curius,
  The bravest son of Rome,   250
Thrice in utmost need sent forth,
  Thrice drawn in triumph home!
Weave, weave, for Manius Curius
  The third embroidered gown;
Make ready the third lofty car,   255
  And twine the third green crown;
And yoke the steeds of Rosea
  With necks like a bended bow,
And deck the bull, Mevania's bull,
  The bull as white as snow.   260

XXX.

"Blest and thrice blest the Roman
  Who sees Rome's brightest day,
Who sees that long victorious pomp
  Wind down the Sacred Way,
And through the bellowing Forum, 265
  And round the Suppliant's Grove,
Up to the everlasting gates
  Of Capitolian Jove.

XXXI.

"Then where o'er two bright havens
  The towers of Corinth frown; 270
Where the gigantic King of Day
  On his own Rhodes looks down;
Where soft Orontes murmurs
  Beneath the laurel shades;
Where Nile reflects the endless length 275
  Of dark-red colonnades;
Where in the still deep water,
  Sheltered from waves and blasts,
Bristles the dusky forest
  Of Byrsa's thousand masts; 280
Where fur-clad hunters wander
  Amidst the northern ice;
Where through the sand of morning-land
  The camel bears the spice;
Where Atlas flings his shadow 285
  Far o'er the western foam,
Shall be great fear on all who hear
  The mighty name of Rome."

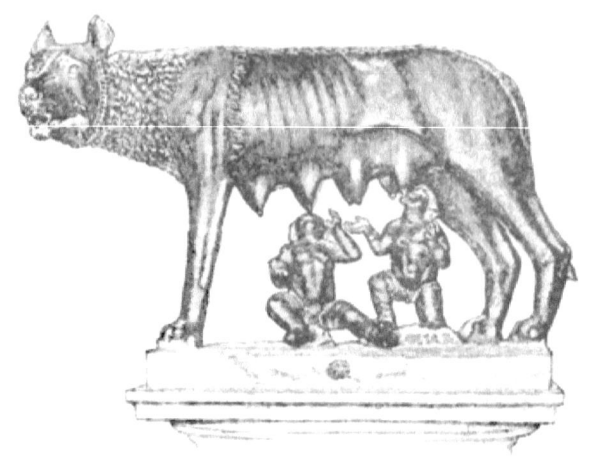

THE BRONZE WOLF OF THE CAPITOL.

NOTES.

N.B. Cf. = compare. *Hor.* = Horatius. *B. L. R.* = The Battle of the Lake Regillus. *Vir.* = Virginia. *P. C.* = The Prophecy of Capys.

HORATIUS.

The year of the city CCCLX: B.C. 391.

1. **Lars:** an honorary title among the Etruscans, like English 'Lord.' — **Clusium:** one of the most important of the twelve cities of the Etruscan Confederation.

2. **Nine Gods:** the nine Great Gods, so called, of the Etruscans, who alone had the power of hurling the thunderbolt.

3. **house of Tarquin:** read in a History of Rome an account of the Tarquins and of the expulsion of the family from Rome.

4. **suffer wrong:** remain in exile, — which was a grievous wrong in the eyes of the Tarquins and their friends.

14. **Etruscan** (or Tuscan): the adjective (here used as a noun) applied to the inhabitants of Etruria (or Tuscia). See map.

19. **amain:** without cessation. Cf. Shakespeare, *3 Henry VI*, II. 1, "to London will we march amain." Other meanings of this word will occur.

25. **Apennine:** the Romans used the singular; we use the plural.

34. Pisae: on the site of the modern Pisa, near the mouth of the Arnus.

36. Massilia: modern Marseilles, early settled by Greeks, and always an important commercial city. — **triremes**: war-ships with three banks of oars.

37. fair-haired slaves: referring to Gauls who had been captured for sale in the Roman market. The Gauls are frequently spoken of as having light-colored hair, in marked contrast with the black hair of the southern nations. Cf. *P. C.* 193-195.

41. diadem of towers: Cortona was built on a very high hill.

45. Ciminian hill: near Lake Ciminus.

47. to the herdsman dear: because its waters were drunk by the "milk-white steers" (cf. l. 55 and *P. C.* 259, 260), a famous breed of oxen much in demand as victims for sacrifice on great occasions.

49. mere: this word is now rarely used except in poetry. It survives in the names of some English lakes, like Windemere.

58-65. old men ... boys ... girls: of course, because the young men were in the army.

61. plunge the struggling sheep: sheep are "plunged" to wash the wool before shearing.

62. vats of Luna, etc.: in allusion to the custom of "treading" the grapes.

63. must: the grape juice before fermenting.

66. thirty chosen prophets: augurs, who interpreted the will of the gods. Cf. note on l. 388.

71. verses: prophecies preserved in verse.

72. traced from the right: i.e. written from right to left, like Hebrew, Persian, and Arabic.

80. Nurscia's altars: Nurtia, or Nortia, was a goddess of the Volscinians, probably the same as the Roman Fortuna.

81. golden shields: the twelve golden shields of Rome. In the reign of Numa a golden shield (of Mars) was said to have fallen from heaven, "and on its continued preservation the continued prosperity of Rome was declared to depend." To prevent this from being stolen, eleven others were made exactly like it, so that no one might know which was the true one, and twelve priests were appointed to take charge of them. Cf. *B. L. R.* 624.

96. Tusculan: from Tusculum, a town of Latium. — **Mamilius**: son-in-law of Tarquin the Proud.

98. yellow: a very common epithet of the Tiber, probably from the color of its sands.

HORATIUS.   127

106. **folk**: most of the editions have "folks." Cf. "folk" in *Vir.* 62.

115. **skins of wine**: wine was transported from place to place in bottles made of leather.

117. **kine**: old plural of 'cow,' now seldom used.

122. **rock Tarpeian**: a precipitous cliff on the Capitoline, overlooking the Tiber, from which in later times traitors were hurled.

126. **Fathers**: senators. The expression "City Fathers" is not uncommon now.

132. **Nor ... nor ... nor**: neither ... nor ... nor.

134. **Verbenna**: "The name is one of Macaulay's own invention; it is not mentioned by any Roman writer" [Rolfe]. — **Ostia**: the seaport of Rome, at the mouth of the Tiber.

136. **Astur**: "another name of Macaulay's invention. There is a Latin word *astur*, meaning a hawk" [Rolfe]. — **Janiculum**: a high hill west of the Tiber, commanding the city; not one of the "seven hills."

138. **I wis**: originally *ywis*, an adverb meaning 'certainly.'

142. **Consul**: chief magistrate of Rome. There were two consuls; see note on *B. L. K.* 82.

144. **gowns**: the *toga*, called 'gown' in the Lays, was the outer garment of a Roman citizen. It was a loose, flowing garment and needed "girding up" when action was demanded of the wearer.

146. **standing**: explained by ll. 148, 149.

151. **straight**: for 'straightway.'

156. Macaulay has been criticised for using "Sir." Does the word seem out of place here?

177. **twelve fair cities**: i.e. of the Etruscan Confederation; see note on l. 1.

180. **Umbrian**: a people of eastern and central Italy.

181. **Gaul**: here refers to the people of northern Italy, or Cisalpine Gaul.

184. **port and vest**: carriage (or bearing) and dress. The word 'vest,' now restricted in meaning, is here used as a general word for 'clothing' or 'dress.'

185. **Lucumo**: the title of an Etruscan prince.

188. **fourfold**: having four layers of hide or metal.

189. **brand**: why should a sword be called (metaphorically) a brand?

192. **Thrasymene**: Lake Thrasymenus (better spelled Trasymenus).

194. **war**: warlike array.

199. **false Sextus**: Sextus Tarquinius, son of Tarquin the Proud.

200. **deed of shame**: the rape of Lucretia.

217. **Horatius**: surnamed Cocles (the one-eyed), was of patrician family, representing the Luceres, one of the original three tribes, the other two being the Ramnian (Ramnes) and the Titian (Tities). See the author's introduction, p. 29, l. 26.

229. **holy maidens**: the Vestal Virgins, whose chief duty it was to keep burning the sacred fire on the altar of Vesta. They were six in number, chosen from the highest families, and held in the highest esteem.

237. **strait**: not 'straight'; cf. l. 440.

242. **Ramnian ... Titian**: see note on l. 217.

253. **For Romans ... in the brave days of old**, etc.: men in all ages are wont to magnify the past at the expense of the present.

262. **spoils were fairly sold**: after the capture of the city of Veii by the Romans under Camillus, large quantities of the booty were distributed among the citizens. Later Camillus was accused of making an unfair distribution, and in consequence of the accusation went into exile.

267. **Tribunes**: officers of the city, who had certain extraordinary powers. They were originally appointed to protect the interests of the plebeians, and were themselves plebeians. — **beard the high**: cf. Scott's *Marmion*,

> " And dar'st thou then
> To beard the lion in his den,
> The Douglas in his hall?"

274. **harness**: armor, an old use of the word; cf. "At least we'll die with harness on our back," Shakespeare, *Macbeth*, V. 5.

277. **Commons**: the common people, plebeians.

304. **Ilva**: the modern Elba, still celebrated for its iron mines.

309. **Nequinum**: afterwards Narnia.

310. **pale waves**: the Nar was noted for its sulphurous waters and white color.

314. **clove**: cf. cleft, *Vir.* 205.

335. **Ostia**: see note on l. 134.

337. **Campania**: a seacoast country, southeast of Latium. — **hinds**: peasants, farm laborers; the word has no connection with 'hind' = 'deer.' Jack Cade's army is described in Shakespeare, *2 Henry VI*, IV. 4, as "a ragged multitude of hinds and peasants."

354. **brand**: see note on l. 189.

355. **none but he**: what part of speech is 'but' here?

360. **she-wolf's litter**: refers to the suckling of Romulus and Remus by a she-wolf. Cf. *P. C.* 37-40.

384. **Mount Alvernus**: a mountain in northern Etruria.

388. **augurs**: official soothsayers, who had charge of the public auspices. The effects of lightning were carefully watched and interpreted by the augurs.

392. **amain**: with all his might. Cf. note on l. 19.

417. **Was none**: note the omission of the expletive 'there.'

440. **narrow way**: cf. "strait path," l. 237.

446. **tide**: always note figurative uses of words. What would be the usual prose word for 'tide'?

465. **As to the highest turret-tops**, etc.: how can such an extravagant statement be justified?

470. **tossed his tawny mane**: explain the figure.

483. **grace**: mercy. Cf. Shakespeare, *Hamlet*, I. 5, "So grace and mercy at your most need help you."

488. **Palatinus**: the hill on which the patricians resided, where the original settlement was. When Macaulay was in Rome in 1838, he wrote in his journal: "I then went towards the river, to the spot where the old Pons Sublicius stood, and looked about to see how my Horatius agreed with the topography. Pretty well: but his house must be on Mount Palatinus; for he would never see Mount Coelius from the spot where he fought." [*Life and Letters*, vol. ii, p. 29.]

492. **father Tiber**: i.e. the river-god. It should be remembered that the early Romans looked upon all objects and phenomena of nature as possessed each by its own invisible spirit or deity.

525. **Bare bravely up his chin**: in a footnote to this line Macaulay quotes from Scott

> Our ladye bare upp her chinne.
>
> *Ballad of Childe Waters.*
>
> Never heavier man and horse
> Stemmed a midnight torrent's force;
>   . . . .
> Yet, through good heart and our Lady's grace,
> At length he gained the landing place.
>
> *Lay of the Last Minstrel*, I.

542. **corn-land ... of public right**: lands belonging to the state consisted mainly of territory taken in war. The various *agrarian laws* that were passed from time to time were concerned with the disposition of the public lands. Cf. l. 261.

545. **Could plough**: i.e. 'could plough around.'

550. **Comitium**: an open space adjoining the forum, in which certain assemblies were held.

561. **the Volscian**: the Volscians were a tribe of Latium, among the most formidable of Rome's enemies in the early period of the republic. Coriolanus is the hero of the Volscian wars.

562. **Juno**: the protectress of women and goddess of childbirth. Cf. Shakespeare, *As You Like It*, V. 4, "Wedding is great Juno's crown."

572. **Algidus**: a mountain of Latium, one of the Alban range.

582, 584. **goodman . . . goodwife**: master and mistress of the house. In Carlyle's letters to his sister he often speaks of her husband as "your Goodman."

THE BATTLE OF THE LAKE REGILLUS.

The year of the city CCCCLI: B.C. 303.

2. **lictors**: attendants upon the higher magistrates — the consul had twelve — who carried as symbols of power bundles of rods called *fasces*, to which axes were added. But the axe was not used inside the city after the downfall of the kings. Cf. *Vir.* 224.

3. **Knights**: members of the equestrian order, wealthy citizens who, at this period of Roman history, served in the cavalry with a horse provided by the state.

7. **Castor**: i.e. the temple of Castor and Pollux (the "Great Twin Brethren"), erected in commemoration of the events recorded in this Lay. — **Forum**: an open place between the Capitoline and Palatine hills, where business was transacted, meetings held, etc.

8. **Mars**: i.e. the temple of Mars, the war-god.

13. **Yellow River**: cf. *Hor.* 98, 466, 470.

14. **Sacred Hill**: *mons sacer*, a hill three miles from the city, near the Anio, to which the plebeians had twice seceded when seeking redress of grievances.

15. **Ides of Quintilis**: the fifteenth day of July. July was the fifth month, March being the first. The name July was given to it by Julius Caesar, when he reformed the calendar.

17. **Martian Kalends**: the first day of March (the month of Mars), when was celebrated the festival called Matronalia in memory of the peace made by the Sabine women between the Romans and the Sabines in the time of Romulus.

18. December's Nones: the fifth of December, when were celebrated the Faunalia, or feast of Faunus, the protecting deity of agriculture and of shepherds, also a giver of oracles.

15-18. Kalends, Nones, Ides: the Romans reckoned the days of the month backwards from these three points, the Kalends being the first, the Nones the fifth, and the Ides the thirteenth, except that in March, May, July, and October the Nones came on the seventh and the Ides on the fifteenth.

20. whitest: most propitious; in allusion to the custom of marking days of good omen in the calendar with white, as unlucky days were marked with black. Cf. ll. 156, 780.

24. from the east: the home of the Twin Brethren may be regarded as Sparta, in southern Greece, where they first received divine honors.

25. Parthenius: a mountain in southern Greece.

27. Cirrha: a town in northern Greece. — **Adria**: the Adriatic sea.

31. Lacedaemon: another name for Sparta.

33. Lake Regillus: regarding the locality of this lake, see the author's introduction, p. 60, l. 23.

63. what time = the time when. — **Thirty Cities**: the Latin cities that took the part of the exiled Tarquins.

78. Of mortal eyes were seen: for this use of 'of' = 'by' cf. "He was seen of Cephas, then of the twelve," *1 Cor.* 15, 5; and "Touching this dreaded sight twice seen of us," Shakespeare, *Hamlet*, I. 1.

82. Consul first in place: "When both consuls were in Rome, each was superior during alternate months." [Gow.]

89. Latines: we now spell it 'Latins.'

91. did his office: i.e. read the proclamation that follows.

96. To bring the Tarquins home: it will be remembered that the whole family of the Tarquins was banished when Tarquin the Proud was dethroned.

114. hied him: cf. *Hor.* 145.

119. Conscript Fathers: the title by which the assembled senate was addressed.

123. choose we: is this equivalent to 'we choose' or to 'let us choose'? — **Dictator**: as here implied the dictator was an extraordinary officer, appointed in times of great danger. He had absolute power for the time being, superseding all other magistrates, but this power lasted for only six months, and generally was resigned as soon as the crisis was passed. The 'Master of the Knights,' or 'Master of Horse,' was his second in command.

125. **Camerium:** an ancient town of Latium taken by Tarquin.

126. **Aulus:** cf. l. 83.

132. **axes twenty-four:** i.e. twenty-four lictors, the number that would be assigned to the two consuls; see note on l. 2. The axes in the *fasces* symbolized the power of life and death.

143. **With boys and with gray-headed men:** cf. *Hor.* 58–65.

145. **hard by:** cf. "fast by," *Hor.* 193.

169. **Witch's Fortress:** the Circeian promontory, said by the Roman poets to have been the abode of Circe, the enchantress.

174. **ghastly priest,** etc.: near Aricia was a celebrated temple of Diana, who was worshipped with barbarous customs; her priest was always a runaway slave, who obtained his office by killing his predecessor in single combat.

179. **buffaloes:** these must not be thought of as resembling the buffaloes of North America.

185. **Laurentian:** about Laurentum.

193. **Mamilius:** see note on *Hor.* 96.

200. **vest:** robe; see note on *Hor.* 184. — **of purple.** . . . **By Syria's dark-browed daughters:** Syria was famous for its purple dyes.

203. **sails of Carthage:** Carthage, on the northern coast of Africa, preceded Rome as the commercial power of the Mediterranean.

209. **false Sextus,** etc.: see notes on *Hor.* 199, 200.

216. **but he:** cf. *Hor.* 355.

217. **A woman:** Lucretia.

225. **So spun she and so sang she:** this line has been called "strangely harsh"; do you find it so?

233. **Tibur:** by metonymy, the place for the people. — **Pedum** . . . **Ferentinum:** ancient towns of Latium that early fell into decay.

236. **Gabii:** the place where, according to tradition, Romulus was brought up.

237. **Volscian:** see note on *Hor.* 561. — **succors:** called "aids" in l. 674.

250. **Apulian:** Apulia was a division of southeastern Italy.

263. **Pomptine fog:** refers to the Pomptine marshes, low land between the mountains and the sea. Macaulay wrote, Jan. 1, 1839: "I shall not soon forget the three days which I passed between Rome and Naples. As I descended the hill of Velletri, the huge Pontine Marsh was spread out below like a sea. I soon got into it; and, thank God, soon got out of it." [*Life and Letters*, vol. ii, p. 41.]

278. **Digentian:** the Digentia was a small affluent of the Anio.

288. **Fidenae**: a city five miles north of Rome, which was frequently at war with Rome.

294. **Calabrian**: Calabria was a district of southeastern Italy.— **brake**: see dictionary.

307. **pruning among his elms**: grape-vines were often trained upon elm-trees.

325. **clients**: dependents, followers; plebeians protected by patricians and bound to render service in return. The relations of patron and client were regulated by law.

347. **Titus**: cf. ll. 249-252.

348. **bestrode**: stood over for protection. In Shakespeare's *1 Henry IV*, V. 1, Falstaff says to the prince: "Hal, if thou see me down in battle, and bestride me, so; 't is a point of friendship."

360. **Julian line**: the same to which Julius Caesar belonged.

362. **Velian hill**: a ridge connecting the Palatine with the Esquiline.

368. **made**: is 'make at' a common expression for 'attack,' 'assault'?

375. **the good house**, etc.: Publius Valerius, elected consul in the first year of the republic, and three times afterwards, received the surname Publicola (Poplicola), "friend of the people," on account of his advocacy of the rights of the plebeians. The Valerius mentioned here was Marcus, his brother.

383. **yeoman**: not used in the sense of 'farmer,' but probably as members of a bodyguard, like "Yeomen of the Guard" of the English sovereign.

408. **wist**: imperfect of 'wit,' know.

412. **gnawed the ground**: mention another common expression similar to this.

416. **Consular**: one who had been consul, an ex-consul.

429. **plumed**: read in two syllables.

439. **as**: as if.— **Apennine**: see note on *Hor.* 25.

441. **battle**: battle-line.

444. **amain**: cf. the meaning here with that in *Hor.* 392; also cf. l. 462.

480. **From Aufidus to Po**: i.e. in all Italy, the Aufidus being in far southern Italy and the Po far to the north.

483. **war**: note the frequent use of this word for 'battle.'

495. **lay on**: cf. the familiar "lay on, Macduff," of Macbeth.

506. **head-piece**: helmet.

513. **spurning**: cf. "and spurning with her foot the ground" in Longfellow's *The Building of the Ship*.

547. Herminia: daughter of Herminius; so Virginia, daughter of Virginius, Julia, daughter of Julius, etc.

557. The furies of thy brother: the Furies, called by the Greeks *Eumenides* or *Erinnyes*, were avenging deities who pursued and punished men for their crimes. Here reference is made to the crime of Sextus Tarquinius towards Lucretia.

568. rich Capuan's hall: Capua was the chief city of Campania (southeast of Latium), noted for its wealth and luxury.

569. knees were loosened: a Homeric expression. The knees were regarded by the ancients as the seat of bodily strength.

572. the bravest Tarquin: cf. ll. 251, 252.

603. Samothracia: an island in the northern part of the Aegean sea, where Castor and Pollux were worshipped.

604. Cyrene: a Greek city in northern Africa.

605. Tarentum: a Greek city in southern Italy.

607. Syracuse: the chief city of Sicily, founded by the Dorian Greeks.

609. Eurotas: a river of Laconia, in southern Greece, on the banks of which was Sparta or Lacedaemon. Cf. ll. 29-32.

619, 620. Ardea . . . Cora: i.e. the men of Ardea and Cora. Cf. ll. 233-236.

623. hearth of Vesta: as typical of Rome itself. Vesta was goddess of the hearth and of family life; also of the city regarded as a family. See note on *Hor.* 229.

624. Golden Shield: see note on *Hor.* 81.

641. battle: i.e. line of battle. Cf. l. 441.

646. Celtic: Gallic, the Po being in Cisalpine Gaul.

649. Sire Quirinus: a name applied to the deified Romulus.

659, 660. Ferentinum . . . Lanuvium: see notes on ll. 233, 619.

674. aids: cf. l. 237.

689. Sempronius Atratinus: cf. l. 141.

692. chair of state: otherwise called the "curule chair," which was in shape something like a camp-stool. Cf. *Vir.* 116, 266.

695. the Twelve, etc.: see note on *Hor.* 81.

699. colleges: the word 'college' here means simply 'body of associates' or 'colleagues,' referring to religious bodies.

716. pricking = spurring, — an antiquated use of the word.

721. Asylum: Romulus is said to have opened an asylum, or place of refuge for people of neighboring states, on the Capitoline hill.

723. the fire that burns for aye: see notes on *Hor.* 229 and l. 623.

724. the shield: see note on *Hor.* 81.

745. Vesta: i.e. the temple of Vesta, "Vesta's fane."

747. the well: a pool or pond in the forum, called the "lake of Juturna."

760. the Dorians: a division of the Greek people, whose chief city was Sparta.

768. Sit shining on the sails: an allusion to the electrical phenomenon now called "St. Elmo's fire," and to the superstition that associated this phenomenon with the Twin Brethren.

774. build we: cf. " choose we," l. 123 and note. — **stately dome**: it is said that Aulus the Dictator during the battle vowed a temple to Castor and Pollux. Such a temple was built in the forum opposite the temple of Vesta.

780-796. The worship of the Dioscuri (another name for the Twin Brethren) was introduced in Rome at an early period, and this festival on the 15th of July was continued for several centuries.

786. Mars: cf. l. 8.

VIRGINIA.

The year of the city CCCLXXXII: B.C. 372.

2. Tribunes: see Introduction, p. 89, and note on *Hor.* 267.

5. fountains running wine: "A familiar touch of fancy in ancient legends, as in those of later times." [Rolfe.]

6. maids with snaky tresses: an allusion, probably, to the story of Medusa, whose beautiful hair was changed to hissing serpents on account of the jealousy of Minerva. — **sailors turned to swine**: Circe the enchantress "turned to swine" some of the followers of Ulysses.

10. the wicked Ten: those magistrates, called Decemvirs, who were appointed in B.C. 451 to codify the laws and to rule the city temporarily. They compiled the "Laws of the Twelve Tables," but afterwards refused to lay down their office, and treated the people in a tyrannical manner.

14. Twelve axes: see notes on *B. L. R.* 2 and 132. The axes were not to be carried with the *fasces* within the city limits.

20. With outstretched chin: what is indicated by this attitude? — **client**: see note on *B. L. R.* 325.

23. lying Greeks: as the expression implies, Romans held the Greeks in light esteem.

24. Licinius: see Introduction, pp. 89, 94.

31. **tablets**: boards smeared with wax for writing, etc.

35. **Sacred Street**: *Via Sacra*, the principal street of ancient Rome, which ran from the Capitol through the forum and beyond.

37. **How for a sport**, etc.: find the story in History of Rome.

38. **Lucrece**: in Latin *Lucretia*, wife of Lucius Tarquinius Collatinus, who was a cousin of the king.

64. **Punic**: Carthaginian.

74. **The year of the sore sickness**: refers to the great plague of B.C. 463. Our ancestors of a century or two ago were wont to speak of such a time as "the time of the great mortality."

76. **augurs**: see note on *Hor.* 388.

81. **there was no Tribune**: all the ordinary offices of state were discontinued on the appointment of the Decemvirs. — **the word of might**: a tribune could by his simple *veto* put a stop to the intended action of any other magistrate. See note on *Hor.* 267.

83. **Licinius**: the tribune who carried the famous Licinian laws, by which the patricians and plebeians were finally reconciled, the latter gaining the right to be elected to the consulship. Cf. l. 24. — **Sextius**: the first plebeian consul.

87. **Icilius**: one of the chief leaders in the outbreak against the Decemvirs. Virginia was betrothed to him.

89. **that column**: which commemorated the victory of the Horatii over the Curiatii in the Alban war during the reign of Tullus Hostilius.

94. **Quirites**: the name by which the Romans were addressed as citizens and civilians.

95. **Servius**: Servius Tullius, the sixth king of Rome, who reformed the constitution. — **Lucrece**: the accent here is on the first syllable. Cf. l. 38. So in Shakespeare's *Twelfth Night*, II. 5, "And silence like a Lucrece' knife."

96. **the great vengeance**: of course referring to the expulsion of the Tarquins.

97. **false sons make red**, etc.: Lucius Junius Brutus, the first consul at Rome, put to death his two sons, who had joined in the attempt to restore the Tarquins.

98. **Scaevola**: "the left-handed," who, on being condemned to be burned alive for an attempt upon the life of King Porsena, thrust his right hand into the flames, and held it there without flinching. Read the whole account in a Classical Dictionary or History of Rome.

102. **Sacred Hill**: see note on *B. L. R.* 14.

104. **Marcian fury**: Caius Marcius Coriolanus, who captured the Volscian town Corioli, was much disliked by the plebeians on ac-

count of his haughty bearing towards them, and was condemned to
exile, B.C. 491. — **Fabian pride**: the Fabian family was one of the most
celebrated of the patrician families for many centuries. Cf. *B. L. R.*
356. The reference here is probably to Kaeso (Caeso) Fabius, whose
troops refused to storm the camp of a defeated enemy, and so to complete their general's victory and entitle him to the honors of a triumph.

105. **Quinctius**: Kaeso (Caeso), son of the famous dictator Lucius
Quinctius Cincinnatus, was a violent opponent of the plebeians, and was
driven into banishment.

106. **the haughtiest Claudius**: the father, or perhaps the grandfather, of Appius, the Decemvir, both of whom were noted for their
active hostility to the plebeians. One of them was "hustled in the
Forum in a riot which had been brought on by his overbearing conduct."

111. **No crier to the polling**, etc.: i.e. no elections were held.

112. **No Tribune**, etc.: see note on l. 81.

115. **holy fillets**: i.e. the priesthood. Fillets were bands of red
and white wool tied with ribbons, worn by priests and vestals. —
purple gown: i.e. gown with a purple border, the *toga praetexta*, worn
by the higher magistrates.

116. **axes**: see notes on l. 14 and *B. L. R.* 2, 132. — **curule chair**:
see note on *B. L. R.* 692. — **the car**: i.e. the triumphal chariot.

117. **press**: impress, force into the army.

120. **usance**: interest on money; the word in this sense is now
obsolete. Shylock, in *The Merchant of Venice*, I. 3, says: "Still have
you rated me about my moneys and my usances."

121. **haggard debtors**: the laws in relation to debtors were very
harsh and uncompromising, and the debtors were mostly plebeians.

124. **holes for free-born feet**: the stocks.

130. **Alban kings**: Alba Longa, the most ancient city of Latium,
is said to have founded Rome. See Introduction to *P. C.*, p. 109, ll. 1-5.

133. **Corinthian mirrors**: Corinth in Greece was at this time a
wealthy commercial city.

134. **Capuan odors**: see note on *B. L. R.* 568. — **Spanish gold**:
Spain was noted for its mineral wealth.

148. **great sewer**: constructed by Tarquin the Elder, and still in
use to this day.

149. **whittle**: knife for slaughtering cattle.

152. **Farewell, sweet child**, etc.: this speech of Virginius is considered by some critics to show Macaulay's weakness in dealing with
the pathetic. It has been called "the weakest part of the poem, and
in marked contrast to the concise and pregnant lines of the narrative

elsewhere." The "contrast" is evident enough; does it show weakness? Following are two contrary opinions on this question: "It is a singular thing that Macaulay, whose sensibility and genuine tenderness of nature are quite beyond doubt, had almost no command of the pathetic.... Macaulay could not hold the more passionate emotions sufficiently at arm's length to describe them properly when he felt them. And when they passed, his imagination did not reproduce them with a clearness available for art. A man on the point of stabbing his daughter to save her from dishonor would certainly not think of making the stagey declamation which Macaulay has put into the mouth of Virginius. The frigid conceits about 'Capua's marble halls,' and the kite gloating upon his prey, are the last things that would occur to a mind filled with such awful passions." [J. Cotter Morison in *English Men of Letters, Macaulay*, p. 117.] "This is the only passage in the volume that can be called — in the usual sense of the word — pathetic. It is, indeed, the only passage in which Mr. Macaulay has sought to stir up that profound emotion. Has he succeeded? We hesitate not to say that he has, to our heart's desire.... This effect has been wrought simply by letting the course of the great natural affections flow on, obedient to the promptings of a sound, manly heart, unimpeded and undiverted by any alien influences, such as are but too apt to steal in upon inferior minds when dealing imaginatively with severe trouble, and to make them forget, in the indulgence of their own self-esteem, what a sacred thing is misery." [Professor Wilson in *Blackwood's Magazine*, vol. lii, p. 819.]

157. **civic crown**: a chaplet of oak-leaves with acorns, presented to a Roman soldier who had saved the life of a comrade in battle and slain his opponent.

182. **Volscians**: see note on *Hor.* 561.

184. **leech**: surgeon. Cf. "leech-craft," l. 119.

193. **the nether gloom**: the under-world, where dwelt the shades (*manes*) of the dead. Cf. l. 127.

200. **Sacred Street**: see note on l. 35.

202. **Ten thousand pounds of copper**: for four or five centuries after the founding of Rome copper was the only metal used for money, and even this, in the early times, was not coined, but passed by weight.

203. **clients**: see note on *B. L. R.* 325.

204. **lictors**: see note on *B. L. R.* 2.

213. **cypress**: an evergreen tree, sacred to Pluto, and a sign of death and mourning.

223. **yeomen**: see note on *B. L. R.* 383.

228. Pincian Hill ... Latin Gate: i.e. remotely to north and south.

232. breaking up of benches: what for?

242. Tribunes: the cry now is for the restoration of the tribunes; see note on l. 81.

249. Caius of Corioli: Caius Marcius Coriolanus; see note on l. 104.

251. yoke: conquered enemies were forced to "pass under the yoke," which consisted of two spears set upright in the ground with a third laid across them. The word "yoke" in l. 256 is used in its more common sense. — **Furius**: Marcus Furius Camillus, the greatest general of his time, who took Veii, and drove out the Gauls from the Roman territory, B.C. 390. He was five times dictator.

257. Cossus: the most celebrated man of this name was Sergius Cornelius Cossus, who (B.C. 428) killed the king of Veii in single combat.

258. Fabius: see second note on l. 104. — **chase**: hunters.

266. put their necks beneath: cf. "High on the necks of slaves," *Hor.* III.

268. staves: sticks or clubs, plural of 'staff.'

269. or staff or sword: either staff or sword.

277. Calabrian: cf. *B. L. R.* 294.

278. Thunder Cape: the promontory Acroceraunium on the coast of Epirus, opposite the Calabrian coast of Italy.

THE PROPHECY OF CAPYS.

The year of the city CCCCLXXIX: B.C. 275.

2. Sylvian: descended from Sylvius (Silvius), son of Ascanius and grandson of Aeneas, to whom and his followers the Romans liked to refer their ancestry. All the Alban kings had the cognomen Silvius.

3. Alba Longa: see note on *Vir.* 130.

4. Aventine: according to one tradition Aventinus was an Alban king, who was buried on the hill which took his name.

7. The children: Romulus and Remus.

8. The mother: Rhea Silvia.

23. the dead are living: in allusion to the supposed death and subsequent discovery of the twins.

25. bloody king: see l. 1.

26. **lying priest**: see l. 5.
27. **raging flood**: the Tiber.
34. **yellow foam**: cf. *Hor.* 98, 466.
37. **The ravening she-wolf**: cf. *Hor.* 360.
48. **grandsire**: Numitor.
58. **horse-hair**: the helmet plume.
71. **holy fillets**: see note on *Vir.* 115.
95. **From head to foot he trembled**: he was becoming inspired with prophetic fervor.
106. **vines clasp many a tree**: see note on *B. L. R.* 307.
110. **Tartessian**: from Tartessus, an ancient town of Spain, probably the same as Tarshish of the Bible. See second note on *Vir.* 134.
112. **Libyan**: African. Libya, the Greek name for Africa, was often used for Africa itself.
115, 116. **Arabia . . . Sidon**: in allusion to the various cosmetics and dyes brought from those places.
123. **sprung from the War-god's loins**: the father of Romulus was said to be the war-god Mars.
125. **From sunrise unto sunset**: does this expression refer to place or time?
128. **and name it by thy name**: it was a popular but erroneous belief that the name Rome was derived from Romulus.
130. **Vesta's sacred fire**: the fire on the altar of Vesta was kept continually burning. See notes on *Hor.* 229, *B. L. R.* 623, 723.
149. **Pomona**: goddess of fruits.
150. **Liber**: ancient Italian divinity, patron of agriculture, later identified with the Greek Bacchus or Dionysus.
151. **Pales**: the divinity of flocks and shepherds.
153. **Venus**: goddess of love.
169. **the soft Campanian**: cf. note on "some rich Capuan's hall," *B. L. R.* 568.
171. **Tyre**: see note on l. 235.
173. **Carthage**: see note on *B. L. R.* 203.
175. **Leave to the Greek**, etc.: the pursuits of sculpture and literature are here considered effeminate in comparison with warlike pursuits.
177-184. As is well known, the Romans for many centuries excelled in all the arts of war.
177. **pilum**: the javelin (the peculiar weapon of the Roman legionary soldier) consisted of a heavy wooden shaft about four feet long, into the end of which was inserted an iron shank about two feet long ending in a barbed or flat heart-shaped point.

184. Jove's eternal fane: on the Capitoline hill.

185. Volscian: see note on *Hor.* 561, and cf. *Vir.* 182.

186. vail: the word means 'to lower,' not 'to cover.' Cf. *Merchant of Venice*, I. 1, "Vailing her high top lower than her ribs."

187. Soft Capua: cf. "soft Campanian," l. 169.

189. Lucumoes: see note on *Hor.* 185. — **Arnus**: a river of Etruria.

190. rods: i.e. the *fasces*, symbols of power; see note on *B. L. R.* 2.

191. proud Samnite: three wars were waged by the Romans against the Samnites, a race of central Italy.

193. Gaul: Rome was destroyed by the Gauls in B.C. 390, but was rebuilt.

195. fair-haired: cf. note on *Hor.* 37.

197. The Greek: what Greek general in particular was "the conqueror of the East"?

The bard now reaches the events which this Lay is intended particularly to celebrate, namely, the war with Pyrrhus, king of Epirus.

200. huge earth-shaking beast, etc.: see Introduction, p. 111, l. 27.

205. Epirotes: men of Epirus, a division of northern Greece.

206. Wedged close with shield and spear: referring to the famous Macedonian phalanx.

209. false Tarentum: see Introduction, pp. 109, 110.

225. great triumph: i.e. the triumphal procession; cf. ll. 181-184.

230. the Red King: the name Pyrrhus is derived from a Greek word meaning 'fire,' and originally meant 'flame-colored' or 'red.'

232. gown washed white: see Introduction, p. 110, l. 18.

235. rich dye of Tyre: Tyre in Syria produced and exported large quantities of a purple or crimson dye obtained from a species of shellfish. Cf. ll. 171, 172, also l. 116.

235-248. It should be remembered that in a triumphal procession the spoils of war were carried before the commander for the people to gaze upon.

249. Manius Curius: see Introduction, p. 111, l. 32.

254. embroidered gown: a general when celebrating a triumph wore the *toga picta*, "embroidered gown," and also the *tunica palmata*, an undergarment with embroidery representing palm-branches.

256. green crown: a wreath of laurel.

257. Rosea: a district of central Italy.

259. the bull: for sacrifice at the altar of Jupiter. — **Mevania**: an ancient town in Umbria, celebrated for its breed of white oxen; cf. *Hor.* 55.

264. Sacred Way: see note on *Vir.* 35.

266. Suppliant's Grove: There were said to be two groves in the depression between the two summits of the Capitoline hill.

269. o'er two bright havens, etc.: the situation of Corinth on an isthmus explains the expression.

271. gigantic King of Day: the famous colossal statue of the sun-god. It is said that at Rhodes (southwest of Asia Minor) there is hardly a day in the year when the sun is not visible.

273. Orontes: the principal river of Syria.

276. dark-red colonnades: made of the "dark-red" Egyptian granite, a specimen of which may now be seen in Central Park, New York.

280. Byrsa: the citadel of Carthage.

283. the sand of morning-land: probably referring to Arabia.

285. Atlas: the mountain in northwestern Africa.

PRONOUNCING VOCABULARY OF PROPER NAMES.

(ENGLISH METHOD.)

NOTE. — ae = e; eu = ū; ia, iu, and the like are generally run together in one syllable; thus Hō-rā′tius = Hō-rā′-shus.

Ā′ dri a
Ae bū′ ti us (t = sh)
Ae gā′ tēs
Ae mil′ i us
Al′ ba Lon′ga
Al bin′ i a
Al ex an′ der
Al′ gi dus
Al′ pīne
Al ver′ nus
Am mi ā′ nus
A mū′ li us
An chi′ sēs
An dro nī′ cus
Ā′ ni ō
An tig′ o nus
Anx′ ur
Ap′ en nīne
Ap′ pi us
A pol′ lō
A pol lo dō′ rus
A pū′ li an
Ar′ de a
A ri′ ci a (rish)
Ar pī′ num
Ar rē′ ti um (t = sh)
Ā′ runs
As′ tur

A sȳ′ lum
A til′ i us
At ra tī′ nus
At′ ti la
Au′ fi dus
Au gus′ tus
Au′ lus
Au′ nus
Au′ ser
Aus′ ter
Av′ en tīne

Bac chī′ a dae
Bac′ chus
Ban dū′ si a (zhi)
Ben e ven′ tum
Brū′ tus
Byr′ sa (Bur)

Çae′ sō
Cā′ i us
Ca lā′ bri an
Cal′ vus
Ca mē′ ri um
Cā′ mers
Ca mil′ lus
Cam pā′ ni a
Cap i to lī′ nus

Cap′ u a
Cā′ pys
Car′ thage
Cas′ tor
Cā′ tō
Cat′ ū lus
Çiç′ e rō
Çil′ ni us
Çi min′ i an
Çin çin nā′ tus
Çin′ e as
Çir′ rha
Clā′ nis
Clau′ di us
Cli tum′ nus
Cloe′ li a
Clū′ si um (zhi)
Cō′ clēs
Co los′ sus
Co mi′ ti um (mish)
Cō′ ra
Cor′ inth
Co rī o lā′ nus
Co rī′ o li
Cor′ nē
Cor nē′ li us
Cor tō′ na
Cor′ vus

Cō′ sa
Cos′ sus
Cras′ sus
Crem′ e ra
Cris′ pus
Croē′ sus
Crus tū mē′ ri um
Cū ri ā′ ti ī (t = sh)
Cū′ ri us
Cur′ sor
Cur′ ti us (t = sh)
Çyp′ se lus
Çȳ rē′ nē

Dē′ ci us (c = sh)
Del′ phī
De moph′ i lus
De mos′ the nēs
Den tā′ tus
Di gen′ ti an (t = sh)
Dī ō ny′ si us (nish)
Dī ō nȳ′ sus
Dī os cū′ rī
Dō mi′ ti an (mish)
Dō′ ri ans
Dū il′ i us

Ē gē′ ri a
El′ va
En′ ni us
Ē pī′ rōtes
Ē trū′ ri a
Ē trus′ can
Eū rip′ i dēs
Eū rō′ tas

Fā′ bi us
Fa bri′ ci us (brish)
Fa lē′ ri ī
Faus′ tū lus
Faus′ tus

Fer en tī′ num
Fi dē′ naē
Flac′ cus
Flā′ vi us
Flō′ rus
Fron tī′ nus
Fū′ ri us

Gā′ bi ī

Ha mil′ car
Han′ nō
Her′ cū lēs
Her min′ i a
Her min′ i us
He rod′ o tus
Hē′ si od (s = sh)
Hō rā′ ti ī (t = sh)
Hō rā′ ti us (t = sh)
Hos til′ i us
Hos′ tus

I çil′ i us
Il′ i ad
Il′ va
I tal′ i cus
Ix ī′ on

Ja nic′ ū lum
Jū′ li us
Jū′ nō

Kaē′ so

Laç e daē′ mon
La nū′ vi um
Lars
Lar′ ti us (t = sh)
Lat er ā′ nus
Lā′ ti an (t = sh)
Lat′ ines

Lau ren′ tum
Lau′ sū lus
La vin′ i um
Lē′ da
Li′ ber
Lib′ yan
Li çin′ i us
Liv′ i us
Lū′ can
Lū′ çe rēs
Lū çil′ i us
Lū ci us (c = sh)
Lū crēce′
Lū crē′ ti a (t = sh)
Lū′ cū mō
Lū′ na
Lus cī′ nus
Lū tā′ ti us (t = sh)
Lys′ i as (lish)

Ma mil′ i us
Mā′ ni us
Man′ li us
Mar cel lī′ nus
Mar′ cus
Mars
Mar′ ti al (shal)
Mas sil′ i a
Max′ i mus
Me ġel′ lus
Me nan′ der
Mē′ ti us (t = sh)
Met′ tus
Me vā′ ni a
Mū′ ci us (c = sh)
Mū raē′ na

Naē′ vi us
Nar
Nē′ pos
Ne quī′ num

No men′ tum
Nor′ ba
Nū′ ma
Nū′ mi tor
Nur′ sci a (shia)

Oc′ nus
Od′ ys sey
Ō ron′ tēs̱
Os′ tia

Pal′ a tīne
Pal′ a ti′ nus
Pā′ lēs̱
Pa pir′ i us
Par mē′ ni ō
Par thē′ ni us
Pa trō′ clus
Pē′ dum
Per i an′ der
Per′ seūs
Pic′ tor
Pī′ cus
Pin′ ci an (c = sh)
Pī′ s̱aē
Plau′ tus
Ple bē′ ian
Plū′ tarch
Pol′ lux
Po lyb′ i us
Po mō′ na
Pomp′ tīne
Pop lic′ o la
Pop ū lō′ ni a
Por′ ci an (c = sh)
Por′ se na
Pos thū′ mi us
Pub′ li us
Pyr′ rhus

Quinc til′ i an
Quinc′ ti us (t = sh)
Quin tī′ lis
Quin′ tus
Qui rī′ tēs̱
Qui rī′ nus

Ram′ ni an
Re ġil′ lus
Reg′ ū lus
Rē′ mus
Rex
Rhē̆′ a
Rhōdes
Rōme
Rom′ ū lus
Rō′ s̱e a

Sā′ bīnes
Sam′ nīte
Sam o thrā′ ci a (c = sh)
Sar din′ i a
Sar pē′ don
Sçačv′ o la
Sē′ i us
Sem prō′ ni us
Ser′ ġi us
Ser′ vi us
Sē′ ti a (t = sh)
Sex tī′ nus
Sex′ ti us
Sex′ tus
Sib′ yl līne
Sic′ ci us (c = sh)
Sī′ don
Sil′ i us
Soph′ o clēs̱
So rac′ tē
Spū′ ri us
Stō′ lō
Sū′ tri um
Syl′ vi an
Syr′ a cūse
Syr′ i a

Taç′ i tus
Ta ren′ tum
Tar pē′ ia
Tar′ quin
Tar tes′ si an (s = sh)
Thĕ oc′ ri tus
Thras′ y mēne
Thū çy̆d′ i dēs̱
Ti′ ber
Ti′ bur
Ti fer′ num
Ti′ ti an (t = sh)
Ti′ tus
To lum′ ni us
Tū′ be rō
Tul′ li a
Tul′ lus
Tus′ cū lum
Tȳre

Ū′ fens̱
Um′ bri an
Um′ brō
Ur′ gō

Va lē′ ri us
Var′ rō
Vē′ iī (yī)
Vē′ li an
Vē li′ traē
Vel lē′ ius
Vē′ nus
Ver ben′ na
Ves′ ta
Vir ġin′ i a
Vir ġin′ i us
Vol a ter′ raē
Vol′ e rō
Vol′ sci an (shan)
Vol sin′ i an
Vol sin′ i um
Vul′ sō

THE ATHENÆUM PRESS SERIES

Issued under the general editorship of
Professor GEORGE LYMAN KITTREDGE, of Harvard University, and
Professor C. T. WINCHESTER, of Wesleyan University.

THE FOLLOWING VOLUMES ARE NOW READY:

Sidney's Defense of Poesy. Edited by Professor ALBERT S. COOK of Yale University. 80 cents.

Ben Jonson's Timber; or Discoveries. Edited by Professor F. E. SCHELLING of the University of Pennsylvania. 80 cents.

Selections from the Essays of Francis Jeffrey. Edited by LEWIS E. GATES of Harvard University. 90 cents.

Old English Ballads. Edited by Professor F. B. GUMMERE of Haverford College. $1.25.

Selections from the Works of Thomas Gray. Edited by Professor WM. L. PHELPS of Yale University. 90 cents.

A Book of Elizabethan Lyrics. Edited by Professor F. E. SCHELLING of the University of Pennsylvania. $1.12.

Seventeenth Century Lyrics. Edited by Professor F. E. SCHELLING of the University of Pennsylvania.

Herrick: Selections from the Hesperides and the Noble Numbers. Edited by Professor E. E. HALE, Jr., of Union University. 90 cents.

Selections from Keats's Poems. Edited by Professor ARLO BATES of the Massachusetts Institute of Technology. $1.00.

Selections from the Works of Sir Richard Steele. Edited by Professor GEORGE R. CARPENTER of Columbia University. Cloth. 90 cents.

Carlyle's Sartor Resartus. Edited by Professor ARCHIBALD MAC-MECHAN of Dalhousie College, Halifax, N.S. $1.25.

Selections from Wordsworth's Poems. Edited by Professor EDWARD DOWDEN of the University of Dublin. $1.25.

Specimens of the Pre-Shaksperean Drama. Edited by Professor JOHN M. MANLY of Chicago University. In three volumes. Vols. I. and II. now ready. $1.25 each.

Selections from Malory's Morte Darthur. Edited by Professor WILLIAM E. MEAD of Wesleyan University, Middletown, Conn. $1.00.

Burke's Speech on Conciliation with America. Edited by Professor HAMMOND LAMONT of Brown University. 50 cents.

Selections from Shelley's Poems. Edited by W. J. ALEXANDER of the University of Toronto. $1.15.

Selections from Landor. Edited by W. B. S. CLYMER, formerly of Harvard University. $1.00.

Selections from William Cowper's Poems. Edited by JAMES O. MURRAY of Princeton University. $1.00.

Selections from Robert Burns's Poems. Edited by the late JOHN G. DOW, formerly of the University of Wisconsin. $1.10.

The Poems of William Collins. Edited by WALTER C. BRONSON of Brown University. 90 cents.

Gibbon's Memoirs. Edited by Professor OLIVER F. EMERSON of Western Reserve University. $1.10.

GINN & COMPANY, Publishers.

BOOKS ON ENGLISH LITERATURE

Athenæum Press Series : 16 volumes now ready
Baldwin's Inflection and Syntax of Malory's Morte d'Arthur $1.40
Browne's Shakspere's Versification   .25
Corson's Primer of English Verse   1.00
Emery's Notes on English Literature   1.00
Frink's New Century Speaker   1.00
Garnett's Selections in English Prose from Elizabeth to Victoria   1.50
Gayley's Classic Myths in English Literature   1.50
Gayley's Introduction to Study of Literary Criticism
Gummere's Handbook of Poetics   1.00
Hudson's Life, Art, and Characters of Shakespeare.   2 vols   4.00
Hudson's Classical English Reader   1.00
Hudson's Text-Book of Prose   1.25
Hudson's Text-Book of Poetry   1.25
Hudson's Essays on English, Studies in Shakespeare, etc.   .25
Kent's Shakespeare Note-Book   .60
Litchfield's Spenser's Britomart   .60
Minto's Manual of English Prose Literature   1.50
Minto's Characteristics of the English Poets   1.50
Phelps' Beginnings of the English Romantic Movement   1.00
Smith's Synopsis of English and American Literature   .80
Standard English Classics : 13 volumes now ready
Thayer's Best Elizabethan Plays   1.25
White's Philosophy of American Literature   .30
White's Philosophy of English Literature   1.00
Winchester's Five Short Courses of Reading in English Literature   .40

GINN & COMPANY, Publishers,

Boston.   New York.   Chicago.   Atlanta.   Dallas.

www.ingramcontent.com/pod-product-compliance
Lightning Source LLC
Chambersburg PA
CBHW022115160426
43197CB00009B/1039